"WE"

Charles A. Lindbergh

"WE"

The Famous Flier's Own Story of His Life
and His Transatlantic Flight, Together
with His Views on the Future of Aviation.

With a Foreword by

Myron T. Herrick
U.S. Ambassador to France

Buccaneer Books
Cutchogue, New York

International Standard Book Number: 0-89966-832-1

For ordering information, contact:

Buccaneer Books, Inc.
P.O. Box 168
Cutchogue, N.Y. 11935

(631) 734-5724, Fax (631) 734-7920
    www.BuccaneerBooks.com

DEDICATED TO

MY MOTHER

AND TO THE MEN WHOSE CONFIDENCE AND
FORESIGHT MADE POSSIBLE THE FLIGHT OF THE

"SPIRIT OF ST. LOUIS"

MR. HARRY H. KNIGHT
MAJOR WILLIAM B. ROBERTSON
MAJOR ALBERT BOND LAMBERT
MR. J. D. WOOSTER LAMBERT
MR. HAROLD M. BIXBY
MR. EARL C. THOMPSON
MR. HARRY F. KNIGHT
MR. E. LANSING RAY

FOREWORD

WHEN Joan of Arc crowned her King at Rheims, she became immortal. When Lafayette risked his all to help the struggling Americans, he wrote his memory forever across a mighty continent. The shepherd boy David in five minutes achieved with his sling a place in history for all time. These three shining names represent the triumph of youth and idealism, and we would not speak of them with such reverence today had their motives been less pure or had they ever for an instant thought of themselves or their place in history. So it was with Lindbergh, and all the praise awarded him, judged by the rigid standards of history and precedent, he has merited. He was the instrument of a great ideal, and one need not be fanatically religious to see in his success the guiding hand of Providence.

For he was needed and he came, came at a moment which seemed exactly preordained. He was needed by France and needed by America and had his arrival been merely the triumph of a great adventure, the influence of his act would have gone no further than have other great sporting and commercial achievements.

There have been moments here in France when all that my eye could reach or my intelligence fathom appeared dark and foreboding and yet, in spite of all, my soul would be warmed as by some invisible sunshine. At such times, when all human efforts had apparently failed, suddenly the affairs of nations seemed to be taken from out the hands of men and directed by an unseen power on high.

Just before the Battle of the Marne I was standing on the river embankment. A great harvest moon was rising over the city near

Notre Dame. It seemed to rest on the corner of a building. The French flag was blowing steadily across its face. In the fleeting moments while this spectacle lasted, people knelt on the quay in prayer. I inquired the meaning of these prayers. The answer was that there is a prophecy centuries old that the fate of France will finally be settled upon the fields where Attila's hordes were halted and driven back, and where many battles in defense of France have been won. And pointing up the Seine to the French flag outlined across the moon, people cried: "See! the sign in Heaven! It means the victory of French arms! The prophecy is come true as of old and France is once more to be saved on those chalky fields."

Now when this boy of ours dropped unheralded from the sky and circling the Eiffel Tower came to rest as gently as a bird on the field of Le Bourget, I was seized with the same premonition as those French people on the quay that August night. I felt, without knowing why, that his arrival was far more than a fine deed well accomplished, and there glowed within me the prescience of a splendor yet to come. Lo! it *did* come and has gone on spreading its beneficence upon two sister nations which a now conquered ocean joins.

For I feel in every fibre of my being that Lindbergh's landing here marks one of the supreme moments in the history of America and France, and the faith we have had in the deciding power of spiritual things is strengthened by every circumstance of his journey, by all his acts after landing, and by the electrical effect which ran like some religious emotion through a whole vast population. The "Spirit of St. Louis" was to the French people another sign come out of the sky—a sign which bore the promise that all would be well between them and us.

France took Charles Lindbergh to her heart because of what he was and because of what she knew he represented. His little ship became the meeting place of the greatest conference that has ever gathered between two nations, for under the shadow of its wings a hundred and fifty million Frenchmen and Americans have come together in generous accord. No diplomatic bag ever carried such a stupendous document as this all-unaccredited messenger bore, and no visiting squadron ever delivered such a letter of thanks as he took up the Potomac in returning. Has any such Ambassador ever been known!

Lindbergh was not commissioned by his government any more than Lafayette was by his, in each case it has merely been left for statesmen to register and approve the vast consequence of their acts. Both arrived at a critical moment and both set in motion those imponderable forces which escape the standards of the politician's mind. Who shall say but what they were God-sent messengers of help, smiling the defiance of their faith at an all too skeptical world? What the one accomplished has already changed history through a century; what the other has just

done the people of America and France will take
good care shall not be wasted.

The way Lindbergh bore himself after getting
here was but a continuation of his flight. He
started with no purpose but to arrive, he remained with no desire but to serve, he sought
nothing, he was offered all. No flaw marked
any act or word, and he stood forth amidst the
clamor and the crowds the very embodiment of
a fearless, kindly, cultivated American youth—
unspoiled, unspoilable. A nation which breeds
such boys need never fear for its future. When
a contract for a million dollars was sent him he
cabled back: "You must remember that this expedition was not organized to make money but
to advance aviation." There is the measure of
his spirit, the key to his intentions.

Flying was his trade, his means of livelihood,
but the love of it burned in him with a fine
passion, and now that his fame will give him a
wider scope of usefulness he has announced that
he will devote himself wholeheartedly to the

advance of aeronautics. His first step in that direction is the publishing of this book, and no one can doubt that its influence will be of enormous value in pushing on man's conquest of the air. It would be idle for me or any one else to estimate now what these results will be, but every American vibrates with a glowing pride at the thought that out from our country has come this fresh spirit of the air, and that the whole world hails Charles Lindbergh, not only as a brave aviator, but as an example of American idealism, character and conduct.

MYRON T. HERRICK

United States Embassy,
Paris,
June Sixteenth, 1927

CONTENTS

A LITTLE OF WHAT THE WORLD THOUGHT
OF LINDBERGH

By FITZHUGH GREEN

13

ILLUSTRATIONS

15

ILLUSTRATIONS 17

"WE"

I

BOYHOOD AND EARLY FLIGHTS

I WAS born in Detroit, Michigan, on February 4, 1902. My father was practicing law in Little Falls, Minnesota, at the time. When I was less than two months old my parents took me to their farm, on the western banks of the Mississippi River two miles south of Little Falls.

My father, Charles A. Lindbergh, was born in Stockholm, Sweden, January 20, 1860, the son of Ola and Louisa Manson. His father (who changed his name to Lindbergh after reaching America) was a member of the Swedish Parliament and had at one time been Secretary to the King.

About 1860 my grandfather with his family embarked on a ship bound for America, and settled near Sauk Center, Minnesota, where he took up a homestead and built his first home in America—a log cabin. It was here that my father spent his early life.

The Rev. C. S. Harrison, writing for the Minnesota Historical Society, gives an account of the activities of my grandfather during the early days in Minnesota.

There were very few schools in Minnesota at that time, and my father's boyhood days were spent mostly in hunting and fishing. His education consisted largely of home study with an occasional short term at country schools.

He was educated at Grove Lake Academy, Minnesota, and graduated from the law school at the University of Michigan, Ann Arbor, with an LL.B. degree.

He began his law practice in Little Falls where he served as County Attorney. He later became interested in politics, and was elected to

FATHER AND SON

MADISON, WISC.—INSTRUCTOR AND CLASSMATES IN A MID-WESTERN MILITARY SCHOOL

the 60th Congress in 1906 to represent the Sixth District of Minnesota at Washington, a capacity in which he served for ten years.

My mother was born in Detroit, Michigan, daughter of Charles and Evangeline Land. She is of English, Irish and French extraction. As a graduate of the University of Michigan, she holds a B.S. degree from that institution, also an A.M. degree from Columbia University, New York City. Her father, Dr. Charles H. Land, a Detroit dentist, was born in Simcoe, Norfolk County, Canada, and his father, Colonel John Scott Land, came from England, and was one of the founders of the present city of Hamilton.

My grandfather was constantly experimenting in his laboratory. He held a number of patents on incandescent grates and furnaces, in addition to several on gold and enamel inlays and other dental processes. He was one of the first to foresee the possibilities of porcelain in dentistry, and later became known as "the father of porcelain dental art."

During the first four years of my life, I lived in our Minnesota home with the exception of a few trips to Detroit. Then my father was elected to Congress and thereafter I seldom spent more than a few months in the same place. Our winters were passed in Washington, and our summers in Minnesota, with intermediate visits to Detroit.

When I was eight years of age I entered the Force School in Washington. My schooling was very irregular due to our constant moving from place to place. Up to the time I entered the University of Wisconsin I had never attended for one full school year, and I had received instruction from over a dozen institutions, both public and private, from Washington to California.

Through these years I crossed and recrossed the United States, made one trip to Panama, and had thoroughly developed a desire for travel, which has never been overcome.

My chief interest in school lay along mechanical and scientific lines. Consequently, after graduating from the Little Falls High School, I decided to take a course in Mechanical Engineering, and two years later entered the College of Engineering of the University of Wisconsin at Madison.

While I was attending the University I became intensely interested in aviation. Since I saw my first airplane near Washington, D. C., in 1912, I had been fascinated with flying, although up to the time I enrolled in a flying school in 1922 I had never been near enough a plane to touch it.

The long hours of study at college were very trying for me. I had spent most of my life outdoors and had never before found it necessary to spend more than a part of my time in study.

At Wisconsin my chief recreation consisted of shooting-matches with the rifle and pistol teams of rival Universities, and in running around on my motorcycle which I had ridden down from Minnesota when I entered the University.

I had been raised with a gun on our Minnesota home, and found a place on the R.O.T.C. teams at the beginning of my freshman year at Wisconsin. From then on I spent every minute I could steal from my studies in the shooting gallery and on the range.

The first six weeks of vacation after my freshman year were spent in an Artillery School at Camp Knox, Kentucky. When that was over I headed my motorcycle south and with forty-eight dollars in my pocket, set out for Florida. After arriving at Jacksonville I started back the same day, but over a different route leading farther west than the first. Seventeen days after leaving Camp Knox I arrived back in Madison with a motorcycle badly in need of repair and nine dollars left in my pocket. After stopping in Madison long enough to overhaul the engine I went to Little Falls to spend the remainder of my vacation.

Soon after the start of my third semester at Wisconsin I decided to study aeronautics in earnest, and if, after becoming better acquainted with the subject, it appeared to have a good future, I intended to take it up as a life work.

I remained at the University of Wisconsin long enough to finish the first half of my sophomore year. Then about the end of March, 1922, I left Madison on my motorcycle en route to Lincoln, Nebraska, where I had enrolled as a flying student with the Nebraska Aircraft Corporation.

The roads in Wisconsin in March, 1922, were not all surfaced and when, after leaving the well-paved highway, I had progressed only about four miles in as many hours, I put my motorcycle on the first farm wagon that passed and shipped it to Lincoln by rail at the next town.

I arrived at Lincoln on the first of April. On April 9, 1922, I had my first flight as a passenger in a Lincoln Standard with Otto Timm, piloting.

N. B. In the following account of flying during the post-war period of aviation, before flying laws and the

Aeronautical Branch of the Department of Commerce came into existence, it should be borne in mind by the reader that the experiences and incidents related in this book in no way describe modern commercial flying conditions. Even in this account it will be noticed that the more spectacular events took place in such a manner that all risk was taken by the pilots and by members of the aeronautical profession; also that exhibition and test flying were responsible for most of these.

In the four emergency parachute jumps described herein, it is apparent that in each case the plane would never have been flown with passengers under the conditions which necessitated the jump.

Commercial air transport has developed rapidly during the last few years, until today it has reached a stage where the safety of properly operated airlines compares favorably with other means of travel.

I received my first instruction in the same plane a few days later under I. O. Biffle, who was known at the Nebraska Aircraft Corporation as the most "hard boiled" instructor the army ever had during the war.

The next two months were spent in obtaining, in one way or another, my flying instruction, and in learning what I could around the factory, as there was no ground school in connection with the flying course at that time.

We did most of our flying in the early morning or late evening on account of the strong Nebraska winds in midday with their corresponding rough air which makes flying so difficult for a student.

I believe that I got more than my share of rough weather flying, however, because my instructor, or "Biff" as we used to call him, had certain very definite views on life, one of which was that early morning was not made as a time for instructors to arise. So as I was the only student and Biff my only instructor, I did very little early morning flying.

By the end of May I had received about eight hours of instruction which (in addition to the $500 cost of my flying course) had required about $150 for train fare and personal expenses.

One morning Biff announced that I was ready to solo, but the president of the company required a bond to cover possible breakage of the plane, which I was not able to furnish. As a result I did not take a plane up by myself until several months later.

Before I had entirely completed my flying course, the instruction plane was sold to E. G. Bahl, who was planning a barnstorming trip through southeastern Nebraska. I became acquainted with Bahl at Lincoln and offered to pay my own expenses if allowed to accompany him as mechanic and helper. As a result we barnstormed most of the Nebraska towns southeast of Lincoln together, and it is to him that I owe my first practical experience in cross-country flying.

"Barnstorming" is the aviator's term for flying about from one town to another and taking any one who is sufficiently "airminded" for a short flight over the country. In 1922 the fare usually charged was five dollars for a ride of from five to ten minutes.

It was while I was flying with Bahl that I began to do a little "wing-walking." We would often attract a crowd to the pasture or stubble field from which we were operating, by flying low over town while I was standing on one of the wing tips.

In June I returned to Lincoln and received a little more instruction, making a total of about ten hours.

About this time Charlie Harden, well known in the aeronautical world for his parachute work, arrived in Lincoln. I had been fascinated by the parachute jumps I had seen, and persuaded Ray Page to let me make a double drop with Harden's chutes.

A double drop is made by fastening two parachutes together with rope. Both are then packed in a heavy canvas bag; the mouth of the bag is laced together and the lace ends tied in a bow knot. The bag is lashed half way out on the wing of the plane, with the laced end hanging down. When the plane has reached sufficient altitude the jumper climbs out of the cockpit and along the wing to the chute, fastens the parachute straps to his harness, and swings down under the wing. In this position he is held to the plane by the bow knot holding together the mouth of the bag containing his parachute, the bag itself being tied securely to the wing. When ready to cut loose he pulls the bow knot allowing the bag to open and the parachute to be pulled out by his weight.

In a double jump, after the first parachute has fully opened, the jumper cuts the rope binding the second chute to the first. The first chute upon being relieved of his weight, collapses, and passes him on the way down.

I made my first jump one evening in June from an 1800-foot altitude over the flying field.

My first chute opened quickly, and after floating down for a few seconds I cut it loose from the second, expecting a similar performance. But I did not feel the comfortable tug of the risers which usually follows an exhibition jump. As I had never made a descent before, it did not occur to me that everything was not as it should be, until several seconds had passed and I began to turn over and fall headfirst. I looked around at the chute just in time to see it string out; then the harness jerked me into an upright position and the chute was open. Afterwards I learned that the vent of the second chute had been tied to the first with grocery string which had broken in packing the parachute, and that instead of stringing out when I cut loose, it had followed me still folded, causing a drop of several hundred feet before opening.

I remained in Lincoln for two weeks working in the Lincoln Standard factory for fifteen dollars a week. Then I received a wire from H. J. Lynch, who had purchased a Standard a few weeks before and taken it on a barnstorming trip into western Kansas. He was in need of a parachute jumper to fill a number of exhibition contracts in Kansas and Colorado, and wanted me to go with him in that capacity at a small fraction of its cost. Page offered me a new Harden Chute instead of my remaining flying instruction, and I took a train for Bird City, Kansas.

Lynch and myself barnstormed over western Kansas and eastern Colorado giving a number of exhibitions from time to time, in which I usually made a jump and did a little wing-walking.

In the fall, together with "Banty" Rogers, a wheat rancher who owned the plane, we set out for Montana. Our course took us through a corner of Nebraska and then up through Wyoming along the Big Horn Mountains and over Custer's Battle Field. At one time in Wyoming we were forced to land, due to motor trouble, near a herd of buffalo, and while Lynch was working on the motor I started over towards the animals to get a picture. I had not considered that they might object to being photographed, and was within a hundred yards of them when an old bull looked up and stamped his foot. In a moment they were all in line facing me with lowered heads. I snapped a picture but lost no

SHIPPING "THE SPIRIT OF ST. LOUIS"

© Donald A. Hall

© *Erickson*

THE MEN WHO MADE THE PLANE. LEFT TO RIGHT: WILLIAM H. BOWLUS, FACTORY MANAGER, RYAN AIRLINES; B. FRANKLIN MAHONEY, PRESIDENT, RYAN AIRLINES; CHARLES A. LINDBERGH; DONALD A. HALL, CHIEF ENGINEER AND DESIGNER; A. J. EDWARDS, SALES MANAGER

time in returning to the plane. Meanwhile Lynch had located our trouble and we took off.

After we had been in Billings, Montana, about a week, Lynch traded ships with a pilot named Reese, who was flying a Standard belonging to Lloyd Lamb of Billings. Lynch and I stayed in Montana while Reese returned to Kansas with Rogers.

We barnstormed Montana and northern Wyoming until mid-October including exhibitions at the Billings and Lewistown fairs.

At the Lewistown fair we obtained a field adjoining the fairgrounds and did a rushing business for three days. We had arranged for the fence to be opened to the grounds and for a gateman to give return tickets to anyone who wished to ride in the plane. All this in return for a free parachute drop.

At Billings, however, our field was some distance from the fair and we decided to devise some scheme to bring the crowd out to us. We stuffed a dummy with straw and enough mud to give it sufficient falling speed to look like a human being.

When the grandstands were packed that afternoon we took off from our field with the dummy in the front cockpit with me. I went out on the wing and we did a few stunts over the fairgrounds to get everyone's attention, then Lynch turned the plane so that no one could see me on the wing and we threw out the dummy. It fell waving its arms and legs around wildly and landed near the Yellowstone River.

We returned to our field and waited expectantly for the curious ones to come rushing out for information, but two hours later, when a few Montanans did arrive, they told us about one of the other attractions—a fellow who dived from an airplane into the Yellowstone River which was about three feet deep at that point. That was the last time we attempted to thrill a Montana crowd.

The barnstorming season in Montana was

about over in October and soon after returning from Lewistown I purchased a small boat for two dollars. After patching it up a bit and stopping the larger leaks, I started alone down the Yellowstone River on the way to Lincoln.

The river was not deep and ran over numerous rapids which were so shallow that even the flat bottom of my small boat would bump over the rocks from time to time. I had been unable to purchase a thoroughly seagoing vessel for two dollars, and very little rough going was required to knock out the resin from the cracks and open the old leaks again.

I had my camping equipment lashed on top of one of the seats to keep it dry, and as I progressed downstream through the ever-present rapids, more and more of my time was required for bailing out the boat with an old tin can, until at the end of the first day, when I had travelled about twenty miles, I was spending fully half of my time bailing out water.

I made camp that night in a small clearing beside the river. There had been numerous showers during the day, which thoroughly soaked the ground, and towards evening a steady drizzling rain set in.

I pitched my army pup tent on the driest ground I could find and, after a cold supper, crawled in between the three blankets which I had sewn together to form a bag.

The next morning the sky was still overcast but the rain had stopped, and after a quick breakfast I packed my equipment in the boat and again started down the river.

The rain set in anew, and this together with the water from the ever-increasing leaks in the sides and bottom of the boat required such constant bailing that I found little use for the oars that day. By evening the rocks had taken so much effect that the boat was practically beyond repair.

After a careful inspection, which ended in the conclusion that further progress was not feasible,

I traded what was left of the boat to the son of
a nearby rancher in return for a wagon ride to
the nearest town, Huntley, Montana. I expressed my equipment and bought a railroad
ticket to Lincoln, where I had left my motorcycle.

A short time before I had left Lincoln, while
I was racing with a car along one of the Nebraska
country roads, a piston had jammed and I had
not found time to replace it. Accordingly, after
returning from Montana, I spent several days
overhauling the machine before proceeding on
to Detroit where I was to meet my mother.

I made the trip to Detroit in three days and
after spending about two weeks there I took a
train for Little Falls to clear up some business
in connection with our farm.

During the winter months I spent part of my
time on the farm and part in Minneapolis with
my father. Occasionally we would drive the hundred miles from Minneapolis to Little Falls together.

In March, 1923, I left Minnesota and after a short visit in Detroit, departed on a train bound for Florida. My next few weeks were spent in Miami and the Everglades.

II

MY FIRST PLANE

SINCE I had first started flying at Lincoln, the year before, I had held an ambition to own an airplane of my own. So when I took my last flight with Lynch in Montana, and started down the Yellowstone, I had decided that the next spring I would be flying my own ship.

Consequently when April arrived, I left Miami and went to Americus, Georgia, where the Government had auctioned off a large number of "Jennies," as we called certain wartime training planes. I bought one of these ships with a new Curtis OX-5 motor and full equipment for five hundred dollars. They had cost the Government nearly twice as many thousands, but at

the close of the war the surplus planes were sold
for what they would bring and the training fields
were abandoned. Americus, Georgia, was a typical example of this. The planes had been auctioned for as little as fifty dollars apiece the year
before. A few days after I arrived, the last officer left the post and it took its place among the
phantom airports of the war.

I lived alone on the post during the two weeks
my plane was being assembled, sometimes sleep-
ing in one of the twelve remaining hangars and
sometimes in one of the barracks buildings. One
afternoon a visiting plane arrived and Reese
stepped out of the cockpit. I had not heard
from him since we had traded planes in Montana,
and he stayed with me on the post that night
while we exchanged experiences of the previous
year.

One of the interesting facts bearing on the life
of aviators is that they rarely lose track of one
another permanently. Distance means little to
the pilot, and there is always someone dropping

in from somewhere who knows all the various
flyers in his section of the country, and who is
willing to sit down and do a little "ground flying" with the local pilots. In this way intimate
contact is continually established throughout the
clan. ("Ground flying" is the term used to
designate the exchange of flying experiences
among airmen.)

I had not soloed up to the time I bought my
Jenny at Americus, although at that time the
fact was strictly confidential.

After my training at Lincoln I had not been
able to furnish the required bond and, although
I had done a little flying on cross country trips
with Bahl and Lynch, I had never been up in a
plane alone. Therefore when my Jenny was
completely assembled and ready to fly I was undecided as to the best method of procedure. No
one on the field knew that I had never soloed.
I had not been in a plane for six months; but
I did not have sufficient money to pay for more
instruction, so one day I taxied to one end of the

field, opened the throttle and started to take off. When the plane was about four feet off the ground, the right wing began to drop, so I decided that it was time to make a landing. I accomplished this on one wheel and one wing skid but without doing any damage to the ship. I noticed that the wind was blowing hard and suddenly decided that I would wait for calmer weather before making any more flights and taxied back to the hangar.

A pilot who was waiting for delivery on one of the Jennies offered to give me a little dual instruction, and I flew around with him for thirty minutes and made several landings. At the end of this time he taxied up to the line and told me that I would have no trouble and was only a little rusty from not flying recently. He advised me to wait until evening when the air was smooth and then to make a few solo flights.

When evening came I taxied out from the line, took one last look at the instruments and took off on my first solo.

The first solo flight is one of the events in a pilot's life which forever remains impressed on his memory. It is the culmination of difficult hours of instruction, hard weeks of training and often years of anticipation. To be absolutely alone for the first time in the cockpit of a plane hundreds of feet above the ground is an experience never to be forgotten.

After a week of practice flights around Southern Field I rolled my equipment and a few spare parts up in a blanket, lashed them in the front cockpit and took off for Minnesota.

This was my first cross country flight alone, less than a week after my solo hop. Altogether I had less than five hours of solo time to my credit. I had, however, obtained invaluable experience the year before while flying around in the western states with Biffle, Bahl, and Lynch.

While learning to fly in Nebraska the previous spring, I discovered that nearly every pilot in existence had flown in Texas at one time or another during his flying career. Accordingly I decided that, at the first opportunity I would fly to Texas myself and although I travelled a rather roundabout way from Georgia to Minnesota, my course passed through Texarkana en route.

The first hop was from Americus to Montgomery, Alabama, and passed over some fairly rough territory of which both Georgia and Alabama have their share.

I had been warned before leaving the field, that the airline course to Texas was over some of the "worst flying country in the south" and had been advised to take either a northern course directly to Minnesota or to follow the Gulf of Mexico. This advice served to create a desire to find out what the "worst flying country in the south" looked like. I had a great deal of confidence in my Jenny with its powerful OX-5 engine, and it seemed absurd to me at that time to detour by airplane. Consequently I laid my route in the most direct line possible to conform with my limited cruising range with forty gallons of fuel.

The flight to Montgomery was uneventful. I landed at the army field there before noon, filled the fuel tanks and took off again for Meridian, Mississippi.

I arrived over Meridian in late afternoon and for the first time was faced with the problem of finding a suitable field and landing in it.

An experienced pilot can see at a glance nearly everything necessary to know about a landing field. He can tell its size, the condition of the ground, height of grass or weeds, whether there are any rocks, holes, posts or ditches in the way, if the land is rough and rolling or flat and smooth; in short whether the field is suitable to land in or if it would be advisable to look for another and better one. In fact, the success of a barnstorming pilot of the old days was measured to a large extent by his artfulness in the choice of fields from which to operate. Often, in case of motor failure, the safety of his passengers, himself, and his ship depended upon his alertness in choosing the best available landing place and his ability in maneuvering the plane into it. If his motor failure was only partial or at high altitude, time was not so essential, as a plane can glide a great distance, either with a motor which only "revs" down a couple of hundred R.P.M. or without any assistance from the engine at all. The average wartime machine could glide at least five times its height, which meant that if it was five thousand feet above the ground the pilot could pick a field to land in five miles away with safety; but if the failure was soon after the take off, then instant decision and immediate action were necessary.

An amateur, on the other hand, has not over-come the strangeness of altitude, and the ground below looks entirely different than it does from the air, although there is not the sensation, in an airplane, of looking down as from a high build-ing. Hills appear as flat country, boulders and ditches are invisible, sizes are deceptive and marshes appear as solid grassland. The student has not the background of experience so essential to the successful pilot, yet his only method of learning lies in his own initiative in meeting and overcoming service conditions.

There was no regular airport in Meridian in 1923, and a few fields available for a reasonably safe landing. After a half hour's search I decided on the largest pasture I could see, made the best kind of a short field landing I knew how by coming down just over the tree tops, with the engine wide open, to the edge of the field, then cutting the gun and allowing the ship to slow down to its landing speed. This method brings the plane in with tremendous velocity and requires a much larger landing field than is necessary, but until the pilot has flown long enough to have the "feel" of his ship it is far safer to come in fast than too slow.

It had been raining at Meridian and the field was a little soft, so that when my "Jenny" finally did settle to the ground it had a very short roll and there was still some clear ground in front.

I taxied up to a fence corner alongside of a small house and proceeded to tie down for the night. I had gained considerable respect for the wind in Kansas and Nebraska, so after turning off the gasoline and letting the motor stop by running the carburetor dry, (a safety expedient to keep the everpresent person who stands directly under the propeller while he wiggles it up and down, from becoming an aeronautical fatality) I pushed the nose of the plane up to a fence and after blocking the wheels securely, tied each wing tip to a fence post and covered the motor and cockpit with a canvas in case of rain.

By this time the usual barnstorming crowd had gathered and I spent the remaining daylight explaining that the hole in the radiator was for the propeller shaft to go through; that the wings were not made of catgut, tin, or cast iron, but of wood framework covered with cotton or linen shrunk to drum tightness by acetate and nitrate dope; that the only way to find out how it feels to fly was to try it for five dollars; that it was not as serious for the engine to stop as for a wing to fall off; and the thousand other questions which can only be conceived in such a gathering.

As night came on and the visibility decreased the crowd departed, leaving me alone with a handful of small boys who always remain to the last and can only be induced to depart by being allowed to follow the aviator from the field.

I accepted an invitation to spend the night in the small house beside the field.

The next morning I telephoned for a gas truck to come out to the field and spent the time before the truck arrived in the task of cleaning the distributor head, draining the carburetor jet wells and oiling the rocker arms on the engine.

While I was working, one of the local inhabitants came up and volunteered the information that he had been a pilot during the war but had not flown since and "wouldn't mind takin' a ride again." I assured him that much as I would enjoy taking him up, flying was very expensive and that I did not have a large fund available to buy gasoline. I added that if he would pay operating costs, which would be five dollars for a short ride, I would be glad to accommodate him. He produced a five dollar bill and after warming up the motor I put him in the cockpit and taxied through the mud to the farthest corner of the field. This was to be my first passenger.

The field was soft and the man was heavy; we stalled over the fence by three feet and the nearest tree by five. I found myself heading up a thickly wooded slope, which was sloping upward at least as fast as I was climbing in that direction and for three minutes my Jenny and the slope fought it out over the fifteen feet of air between them. Eventually, however, in the true Jenny style we skimmed over the hilltop and obtained a little reserve altitude. I had

ST. LOUIS, MO.—FINANCIAL BACKERS OF THE NON-STOP NEW YORK TO PARIS FLIGHT

UPPER ROW, LEFT TO RIGHT: HAROLD M. BIXBY, HARRY HALL KNIGHT, HARRY F. KNIGHT, MAJOR A. B. LAMBERT

LOWER ROW, LEFT TO RIGHT: J. D. WOOSTER LAMBERT, MAJOR WILLIAM B. ROBERTSON, E. LANSING RAY, EARL C. THOMPSON

FUSILAGE FRAME OF THE PLANE

—BY DONALD A. HALL

passed through one of those almost-but-not-quite accidents for which Jennies are so famous and which so greatly retarded the growth of commercial flying during the post-war period.

I decided that my passenger was entitled to a good ride after that take-off and kept him up chasing a buzzard for twenty minutes. After we landed he commented on the wonderful take-off and how much he enjoyed flying low over the treetops; again assured me that he had flown a great deal in the war; and rushed off to tell his friends all about his first airplane ride.

The gasoline truck had arrived and after servicing the ship I took off again and headed west. I had no place in mind for the next stop and intended to be governed by my fuel supply in picking the next field.

The sky was overcast with numerous local storms. I had brought along a compass, but had failed to install it on the instrument board, and it was of little use in a suitcase out of reach. The boundary lines in the south do not run north and

south, east and west as they do in the Northern
states but curve and bend in every conceivable
direction, being located by natural landmarks
rather than meridians and parallels. I was flying by a map of the entire United States, with
each state relatively small.

I left Meridian and started in the direction of
Texas, cutting across country with no regard
for roads or railways. For a time during the
first hour I was not sure of my location on the
map, but soon passed over a railway intersection
which appeared to be in the proper place and
satisfied me about my position. Then the territory became wilder and again I saw no check-
points. The storm areas were more numerous
and the possible landing fields farther apart, until near the end of the second hour I decided to
land in the first available field to locate my
position and take on more fuel. It required
nearly thirty more minutes to find a place in
which a plane could land and take-off with any
degree of safety, and after circling the field sev-

eral times to make sure it was hard and contained no obstacles, I landed in one corner, rolled down a hillside, taxied over a short level stretch, and came to rest half-way up the slope on the far side of the field.

A storm was approaching rapidly and I taxied back towards the fence corner at rather high speed. Suddenly I saw a ditch directly in front of me and an instant later heard the crash of splintering wood as the landing gear dropped down and the propeller came in contact with the ground. The tail of the plane rose up in the air, turned almost completely over, then settled back to about a forty-five degree angle. My first "crack-up"!

I climbed out of the cockpit and surveyed the machine. Actually the only damage done was to the propeller, and although the wings and fuselage were covered with mud, no other part of the plane showed any marked signs of strain. I had taxied back about thirty feet east of the landing tracks and had struck the end of a grass-covered ditch. Had I been ten feet farther over, the accident would never have happened. The usual crowd was assembling, as the impact of the "prop" with the ground had been heard in all of the neighboring fields and an airplane was a rare sight in those parts.

They informed me that I was halfway between Maben and Mathiston, Mississippi, and that I had flown one hundred and twenty-five miles north instead of west.

When enough men had assembled we lifted the plane out of the ditch, pushed it over to a group of pine trees and tied it down to two of the trees. After removing all loose equipment I rode into Maben with one of the storekeepers who had locked up his business when he heard about the landing of the plane.

I wired Wyche at Americus to ship me one of the two propellers I had purchased before leaving, then engaged a room at the old Southern Hotel.

While waiting for the propeller I had extracted promises from half a dozen citizens to ride at five dollars each. This would about cover the cost of the "prop," as well as my expenses while waiting for it to arrive. When it did come I put it on the shaft between showers, with the assistance of most of Maben and Mathiston. I gave the plane a test flight and announced that I was ready to carry passengers when it was not raining too hard.

The Mississippians who were so anxious to fly when the propeller was broken immediately started a contest in etiquette. Each and every one was quite willing to let someone else be first and it required psychology, diplomacy, and ridicule before the first passenger climbed into the cockpit. I taxied over to the far corner of the field, instructed my passenger how to hold the throttle back to keep the ship from taking off, and lifted the tail around in order to gain every available foot of space for the take-off.

The first man was so audibly pleased with his

ride that the others forgot their manners of a few minutes before and began arguing about who was to be next.

That afternoon a group of whites chipped in fifty cents apiece to give one of the negroes a hop, provided, as they put it, I would do a few "flip flops" with him. The negro decided upon was perfectly willing and confident up to the time when he was instructed to get in; even then he gamely climbed into the cockpit, assuring all of his clan that he would wave his red bandanna handkerchief over the side of the cockpit during the entire flight in order to show them that he was still unafraid.

After reaching the corner of the field I instructed him, as I had the previous passengers, to hold the throttle back while I was lifting the tail around. When I climbed back in my cockpit I told him to let go and opened the throttle to take off. We had gone about fifty yards when it suddenly occurred to him that the ship was moving and that the handle he was to hold on to was not where it should be. He had apparently forgotten everything but that throttle, and with a death grip he hauled it back to the closed position. We had not gone far enough to prevent stopping before reaching the other end of the field and the only loss was the time required to taxi back over the rough ground to our starting point. Before taking off the next time, however, I gave very implicit instructions regarding that throttle.

I had promised to give this negro a stunt ride yet I had never had any instruction in aerobatics. I had, however, been in a plane with Bahl during two loops and one tailspin. I had also been carefully instructed in the art of looping by Reese who, forgetting that I was not flying a Hisso standard with twice the power of my Jenny, advised me that it was not necessary to dive excessively before a loop but rather to fly along with the motor full on until the plane gathered speed, then to start the loop from a level flying position.

I climbed up to three thousand feet and started in to fulfill my agreement by doing a few airsplashes, steep spirals and dives. With the first deviation from straight flight my passenger had his head down on the floor of the cockpit but continued to wave the red handkerchief with one hand while he was holding on to everything available with the other, although he was held in securely with the safety belt.

Finally, remembering my ground instructions, I leveled the plane off and with wide open motor waited a few moments to pick up maximum speed, then, slowly pulling back on the stick I began to loop. When I had gotten one-fourth of the way around, the ship was trembling in a nearly stalled position; still, the Curtiss motor was doing its best and it was not until the nose was pointing directly skyward at a ninety degree angle that the final inertia was lost and for an instant we hung motionless in the perfect position for a whipstall. I kicked full right rudder immediately to throw the plane over on its side but it was too late, the controls had no effect.

The negro meanwhile decided that the "flip flops" were over and poked his head over the side of the cockpit looking for mother earth. At that instant we whipped. The ship gathered speed as it slid backwards towards the ground, the air caught the tail surfaces, jerked them around past the heavier nose and we were in a vertical dive; again in full control, but with no red handkerchief waving over the cockpit. I tried another loop in the same manner but just before reaching the stalling point in the next one I kicked the ship over on one wing and evaded a whipstall. After the second failure I decided that there must be something wrong with my method of looping and gave up any further attempt for that afternoon. But it was not until we were almost touching the ground that the bandanna again appeared above the cowling.

I remained in Maben for two weeks carrying over sixty passengers in all or about three hundred dollars worth. People flocked in from all over the surrounding country, some travelling for fifteen miles in oxcarts just to see the plane fly.

One old negro woman came up and asked,—

"Boss! How much you all charge foah take me up to Heaben and leave me dah?"

I could have carried many more passengers but it rained nearly every day and each flight rutted the field badly. When I landed it was necessary to pass over a soft spot between two hillsides, and before taking off I had to taxi back over this soft place on the way to the far corner of the field. During the last few days several men were required on each wing to push the plane through the mud to the hillside beyond. Another difficulty was that the old black war-time rubber shock absorber card had deteriorated to such an extent that I replaced it with hemp rope and taxi-ing over the harder parts of the field was a very rough procedure, especially since the ground had been plowed in years gone by and allowed to grow sod without being harrowed.

I made several attempts to find another suitable field nearby but there was none from which I could safely operate.

Landing fields are of primary importance to safety in aviation. It is not a question of how small a field a plane can operate from, but rather of how large a field is necessary to make that operation safe.

Large and well equipped airports situated close to cities will go far towards developing commercial airlines and keeping the United States at the top in aeronautical activity.

The cities who foresee the future of air transportation and provide suitable airports will find themselves the center of airlines radiating in every direction.

When an airline is organized, one of the primary considerations is the condition and location of the various landing fields where terminals are contemplated. If the airport is small and in poor condition, or if a passenger must of necessity spend nearly as much time in traveling from the business district out to the field as it will require for him to fly from the field to his destination, then it is very probable that some other city will be selected for the stopping point.

The condition of the field together with the fact that after a heavy rain it was often necessary to carry gasoline in five gallon cans a mile and a half over the railroad tracks by hand forced me to leave Maben and a large number of would be passengers behind, and early one morning I took off for the last time and again headed for Texas.

III

I HAD strayed over a hundred miles off my course and experienced a minor crack-up, but I departed with two hundred and fifty more dollars in my pocket than I had arrived with, besides confidence in my ability to make at least a little more than expenses by barnstorming.

The constant rains had filled the rivers to overflowing, and after leaving Maben I flew over flooded territory nearly all the way to Lake Village, Arkansas. Often the water was up to the second story windows of the farmhouses, and a forced landing at any time would have at least meant nosing over.

I had installed the compass while waiting for

the new propeller at Maben, and experienced no further difficulty in holding my course.

After circling Lake Village I landed in a field several miles north of town. The nearest building was a clubhouse and soon the keeper and his family had arrived beside the plane. They invited me to stay with them as long as I wished, but the keeper persistently refused to accept a flight in return for his hospitality. I carried only a handful of passengers that afternoon. The flying territory around that part of the country was fairly good and there were a number of fields available for planes to land in. Consequently an airplane was no longer the drawing attraction that it was farther in the interior.

I staked the plane down much earlier than usual and went over to the clubhouse.

Evening came on with the clearness of a full moon and open sky. The landscape was illuminated with a soft yellow light; an ideal night for flying. I decided to see what the country looked like from the air at night and jokingly asked my host to accompany me. To my surprise he willingly agreed. For some reason he had no fear of a night flight although I had been unable to persuade him to go up with me in the daytime. What his reaction would have been, had he known that I had never flown after dark before, is a matter of speculation.

We untied the plane, removed the canvases from engine and cockpit, and after a few minutes spent in warming up the motor, taxied down the field and took off for a moonlight flight down the Mississippi and over Lake Village.

Later in the evening after the ship was again securely staked to the ground and we were sitting quietly in the clubhouse, my host stated that he had never spent a more enjoyable quarter of an hour in his life.

The next morning I was again heading towards Texas against a strong westerly wind which retarded the speed of the Jenny so greatly that even with my double fuel capacity it was necessary to land at Farmerville, Louisiana, to replenish my supply. From there I flew to Texarkana and landed between the stumps of the 1923 airport.

On the following morning I left Texarkana with a strong tail wind and after crossing the western end of the Ozark mountains, landed near a small town in north eastern Oklahoma where I took on a fresh supply of fuel and again headed north towards Lincoln, Nebraska.

My tanks began to run low about half way through Kansas and I picked out a hillside near Alma. After flying low and dragging the field several times I came in for a landing, but just as the wheels were about to touch the ground I discovered that it was covered with fairly large rocks half hidden in the tall grass. I opened the throttle to take off but the plane had lost too much speed for the motor to take effect and as it struck the ground the left wing hooked in the rocks and groundlooped the ship to the left but without doing serious damage. The landing gear wires were strained and about two feet of

© *Erickson*

WORKING ON NAVIGATION CHARTS FOR FLIGHT

INSTRUMENT BOARD OF THE PLANE

the rear spar on the lower left wing tip was snapped off. Nothing was broken however which would require immediate repairing.

The field was quite a distance from Alma and in order to get an early start in the morning I stayed with the ship that night. During the heavy rains at Maben, Mississippi, I had constructed a hammock of heavy canvas which could be suspended under the top wing.

I tied the corners of this hammock to the upper strut fittings and crawled into the three blankets inside which were sewn up to form a bag. Thus I spent a comfortable night.

When I arrived over Lincoln the next day I circled over the Lincoln Standard factory, and after landing on the old flying field south of town, waited for the car which was sent out to bring in visiting airmen.

The remainder of the day was spent in "ground flying" with my friends in the factory. We had not been together for seven months and the usual exchange of experiences was necessary.

I soon learned that Bud Gurney had made a parachute for himself and was intending to test it by the simple method of going up to an altitude of fifteen hundred or two thousand feet and cutting loose from the plane. If the chute opened it was successful.

After a great deal of persuasion I prevailed upon him to let me take him up in my ship while we made the first test with a sand bag.

The tanks had just been filled with fuel but I had unlimited confidence in my Jenny and we lashed the parachute and a sandbag on the right wing. Bud, who weighed one hundred and sixty-five pounds himself, climbed into the front cockpit and we started to take-off with a total load of about six hundred pounds, to say nothing of the resistance of the parachute and sandbag which were directly in the slipstream from the propeller.

Even with this load we cleared the nearest obstacle by a safe margin and finally attained an altitude of about two hundred feet. Then we were caught by a descending current of air which carried the plane down to within ten feet of the ground, and try as I would I could not get any higher. A wooded hill was directly in front, and to avoid striking the trees I turned down wind. A railroad trestle was then in front of us and we stalled over it by inches. For five minutes we dodged hills, trees, and houses. I signaled Bud to cut the sandbag, but when he started to climb out of the cockpit to reach it, the added resistance brought the plane down still lower. Then in front of us appeared a row of trees, much higher than the rest, which I knew it would not be possible to get over. We were then passing over a grain field and I cut the gun and landed down wind. The grain was high enough to keep the ship from rolling far and we unloaded the sandbag before taking off again. With the weight of the bag and its resistance gone, we had no trouble in getting out of the grain and back to the flying field.

A week later Bud carried out his original intention of testing the chute. It was successful.

Before continuing the flight to Minnesota, Bud and I made a short barnstorming trip through eastern Nebraska. That territory had been fairly well covered by other barnstormers, however, and we did very little business.

At one place where we landed we were overtaken by a violent thunderstorm combined with a strong wind. It came up so suddenly that we had only time enough to tail the ship into the wind and lash the stick to keep the ailerons from whipping before the wind struck us. We were both holding on to the tail trying to keep the plane from blowing away. Following the wind was a heavy rain which covered the ground with water and at each flash of lightning the electricity on the wires of the ship would pass to the ground through our bodies with the intensity of a booster magnet.

In an electric storm a plane acts as part of a condenser, since it is insulated from the ground by the rubber tires and wooden tailskid. It is possible to receive a violent shock by standing on wet ground and holding on to one of the wires.

We were unable to let go of the ship in the high wind and could only remain and take these discharges as they came. Fortunately the storm did not last long.

The night after our return to Lincoln we slept on the field so that I could get a good start in the morning. Bud was in the back of a Ford truck, and I was in the hammock.

The next morning was overcast with local showers which were visible in every direction. I took off soon after daybreak and after flying through several storms landed in a hayfield at Forest City, Iowa, where I serviced the ship between showers and took off on the final flight to Shakopee, Minnesota, where I expected to meet my father and carry him around on his campaign.

I found Shakopee covered by a cloudburst and in flying around waiting for the storm to pass so that I could land I got into a heavy shower near Savage. One of the cylinders cut out, and I was circling preparatory to landing in a clover field when two more stopped firing. I was flying at less than a two hundred foot altitude and losing that rapidity. It was necessary to land immediately but the only choice of landing places lay between a swamp and high trees. I took the swamp and cut the throttle. When the wheels touched earth they rolled about twenty feet, sank into the spreader bar and we nosed over.

The rudder did not quite touch the swamp grass and the plane stopped after passing through three-quarters of a semi-circle, with the radiator cap and top wing resting on the ground. I was hanging on the safety belt but when I tried to open the clasp with one hand, holding on with the other to keep from falling out on my head, I found it to be jammed. After several futile attempts to open it I reverted to the two strap buckles at the end of the belt to release myself from the cockpit.

All this required not more than two or three minutes.

After getting out of the cockpit I inspected the plane carefully. Again there was little actual damage. The propeller was badly cracked and would have to be replaced; there was a crack in the spreader board which required winding with strong cord. Otherwise the plane was in perfect condition although splashed with mud.

For once there was no one in sight and I made my way through the swamp to the nearest farm-house. On the way I found that there was solid ground along the edge of the swamp less than 100 yards from the plane from which I could take off.

The farmer had seen the plane pass over in the rain and was on his way down towards the swamp when I met him. He informed me that it was not possible to get horses through the mire out to the ship and that he had no idea of how I was to get it back to hard sod again.

I borrowed a rope from him to use in pulling

the tail back to a normal position and we started back to the swamp.

Meanwhile it seems that two boys had seen me land, and when I did not emerge from the cockpit immediately, had run to Savage with the news that "an aviator had landed upside down in the swamp" and that they had "gone up and felt of his neck and that it was stiff and he was stone dead."

I had flown over the town in the rain only a few minutes before, and as in those days it was not difficult for any one to believe anything about an airplane, the town promptly locked its doors and came crawling and wading through the swamp. The older inhabitants followed the railroad track around its edge and by the time I returned with the farmer and a rope there were enough townspeople to solve my problem by carrying the ship back onto solid ground.

They were undoubtedly much disappointed at having come so far on a false alarm but turned to willingly to help me get the ship out of the swamp.

The next edition of one of the Minneapolis papers carried the following item which typically exemplifies what has been the average man's knowledge of aeronautics.

AIRPLANE CRASHES NEAR SAVAGE

Charles A. Lindbergh, son of ex-Congressman Lindbergh, crashed near Savage, Minnesota, this morning. He was flying in his plane three hundred feet above the ground when it suddenly went into a nose dive and landed on its propeller in a swamp. Lindbergh says he will be flying again in three days.

After reading this and similar accounts of equally minor accidents of flight, it is little wonder that the average man would far rather watch some one else fly and read of the narrow escapes from death when some pilot has had a forced

landing or a blowout, than to ride himself. Even
in the post-war days of now obsolete equipment,
nearly all of the serious accidents were caused
by inexperienced pilots who were then allowed
to fly or to attempt to fly—without license or restriction about anything they could coax into
the air—and to carry any one who might be be-
guiled into riding with them.

My next move was to wire to Little Falls for
a propeller which Wyche had expressed from
Americus and two days later joined my father
in his campaign at Marshall.

My father had been opposed to my flying from
the first and had never flown himself.   However, he had agreed to go up with me at the first
opportunity, and one afternoon he climbed into
the cockpit and we flew over Redwood Falls together.   From that day on I never heard a word
against my flying and he never missed a chance
to ride in the plane.

After the campaign was over I spent the remainder of the summer barnstorming through

Minnesota, northern Iowa and western Wisconsin. Most of the time I was alone, but I took one student around with me for a few weeks while I was teaching him to fly, and then I barnstormed southern Minnesota with my mother for ten days. My mother had never objected to my flying, and after her first flight at Janesville, Minnesota, she became an enthusiast herself.

We had been together constantly up to the start of my flying career and had both looked forward to flying around together. Consequently when the opportunity presented itself I wired her to meet me at Janesville.

My mother enjoyed flying from the first and has made a number of flights with me; including a round trip between Chicago and St. Louis in the mail compartment of my plane.

Some weeks I barely made expenses, and on others I carried passengers all week long at five dollars each. On the whole I was able to make a fair profit in addition to meeting expenses and depreciation.

One evening while I was waiting for chance passengers at a field in southern Minnesota, a car drove up with several young fellows in it, one of whom was a graduate of the Army Air Service Training Schools. He asked me why I did not apply for enlistment as a cadet at Brooks Field and explained that by writing to the Chief of Air Service at the War Department in Washington I could get enrollment blanks and full information on the course and its requirements.

I had always wanted to fly modern and powerful planes. Ever since I had watched a group of fourteen DeHavilands with their four hundred horsepower Liberty motors come into the field at Lincoln in my flying school days, I had longed to fly one of them. The Army offered the only opportunity, for there were no Liberty engines flying around barnstorming. Consequently at the hotel that night I wrote my letter to the Chief of Air Service, and a few days later when I received my next mail forwarded from Minneapolis, a letter from Washington with the enrollment blanks was included. The letter informed me that a candidate must be between twenty and twenty-seven years of age inclusive, unmarried, of good physical condition, and must have a high school education or its equivalent.

I completed and returned the forms, and a short time later received another message authorizing me to appear before an examining board at Chanute Field, Rantoul, Illinois, in January, 1924.

Toward the end of September I began to work south. Cold weather was coming on in Minnesota and most people did not enjoy flying in an open cockpit in winter.

I barnstormed over into Wisconsin but found that some one had been carrying passengers for half price there. I had always conformed to the rule in use among most pilots at that time, of giving a good ride for five dollars but not carrying any one for less. So I left southern Wisconsin and turned towards Illinois. After taking off I decided to take in the International Air

Races at St. Louis, which were then in progress;
so instead of sizing up each town I passed over
for its passenger possibilities, I flew towards St.
Louis until the gasoline ran low, then landed,
took on a fresh supply from a passing gas truck,
and pressed on to Carlinville, Illinois. There
I picked up more fuel, and a twenty-five dollar
passenger for St. Louis.

As we neared Lambert Field where the races
were being held we passed over the race course
while the bombers' contest was in progress. I
landed on a hill east of Lambert in order to keep
out of the way of the races, and waited until
evening before hopping over and staking my
ship down at the end of one of the long rows of
civilian planes.

A large number of my old friends were attending the races and soon after landing I met
Bud Gurney who, together with one of the flying
students at Lincoln, had managed to get to the
races without buying a Pullman ticket. He
had brought his chute with him and was entered

in the parachute spot landing contest, in which he was to be the last attraction of the meet by staging a double drop.

In the evening, after the races were over for the day, I carried a few passengers and looked over the different types of planes. I would have given the summer's barnstorming profits gladly in return for authority to fly some of the newer types, and I determined to let nothing interfere with my chance of being appointed a Flying Cadet in the Army. This appeared to be my only opportunity to fly planes which would roar up into the sky when they were pointed in that direction, instead of having to be wished up over low trees at the end of a landing field.

When I went to St. Louis it was with the expectation of pressing on still farther south when the races were over, but with Bud's assistance I sold my Jenny to his friend, flying instruction included. Marvin Northrop who had flown a Standard down from Minneapolis had sold his ship in St. Louis also; together with a course in flying. Since it was necessary for him to return home immediately, I agreed to instruct his student while mine was learning on the Jenny.

I had promised to carry Bud for his last jump, and towards evening on the final day of the races he packed his two chutes and tied them together with the only rope he could find. It was rather old but we decided that it would hold and if it did not the only consequence would be a little longer fall before the second chute opened.

I coaxed the old Jenny up to seventeen hundred feet and as we passed to the windward of the field Bud cut loose. The first chute opened at once, but in opening, the strain on the old rope was too great and it snapped releasing the second chute which fell another two hundred feet before opening.

Planes were circling all around the parachute and flying in every direction without apparent regard for one another. The air was kept in constant motion by their propellers, and the chute swung from side to side in the rough currents

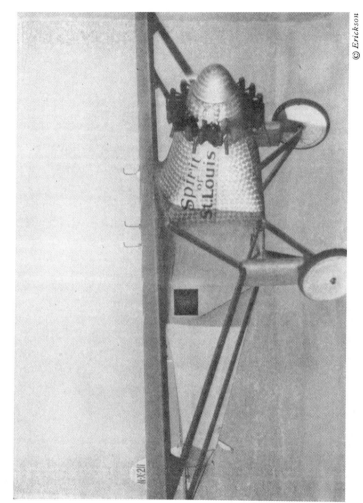

© *Erickson*

"WE" MAKE A TEST FLIGHT

CURTISS FIELD, L. I.—PATSY, THE MASCOT FOR "THE SPIRIT OF ST. LOUIS"

with the result that Bud broke an arm as he landed among the crowd on the side of a ditch. This was the only accident in which any one was injured during the entire meet.

For the next few weeks I instructed my two students and made a short barnstorming tour through Illinois.

IV

WHEN the period of instruction was completed I flew the old Jenny up to my student's home in Iowa and, after watching him make a few solo flights from his home field, I left on a train for Lincoln. My last sight of the old Jenny was as it passed two hundred feet over the station near the center of town—and my parting instruction had been to keep a safe gliding angle when over the city and under no circumstances to come below fifteen hundred feet.

I went to Lincoln to get an S.V.A., which is a two-place Italian pursuit plane, and fly it back to St. Louis. But on arriving I learned that it was in the old Pulitzer Field near Omaha and

84

in questionable condition. It was reported that some cows had eaten all the fabric off the rudder. Cows and mules are fond of the fabric covering, and it is not uncommon to hear of a plane being completely stripped by these animals in a few minutes. On the other hand, I have left a machine unguarded in the same pasture with cattle for days without having them touch it. And during the two weeks I spent at Maben, Mississippi, there had been a number of mules in the same pasture with my ship yet they apparently never came near it.

We filled the back of a touring car with a new rudder and other spare parts, and drove to Omaha the next morning.

The S.V.A. was in even worse condition than had been represented. In addition to needing a new rudder, part of the lock-stitching had broken in the wings and as a result, the fabric was very loose. The radiator had developed a number of leaks which some one had attempted to stop by dumping in a pailful of bran. And when we eventually did get it started the engine skipped badly and would not "rev" up over 1100 R.P.M.

At last we decided to attempt to fly the ship to Lincoln where it would be much more convenient to work on it, and I took off with a sputtering motor and with the centigrade five degrees below boiling. At the end of five minutes the needle was crowding the peg at 115°, and in fifteen minutes the water expansion tank exploded. I landed in a stubblefield and hired the farmer to hitch his team to the ship and haul it to a fence corner next to his house, where I left it to be taken apart and hauled to Lincoln by truck.

I passed the month of December barnstorming in Illinois, and in January went to Chanute Field to take the entrance examinations for a Flying Cadet.

On one occasion while at Lambert Field I had made a short flight into the Ozark foothills with Leon Klink, an automobile dealer who had bought a Canuck that fall and was just learning to fly it. After I returned from Chanute Field and was waiting for the results of my examinations, we decided to make a pleasure flight through the south, barnstorming only enough to make current expenses, if possible. Klink wanted to learn to fly, and at the same time take a vacation, while my only objective was to keep flying and at the same time be ready to enter the next class at Brooks Field which commenced in March, providing my examinations had been passed satisfactorily.

Accordingly on the twenty-third of January we took off from Lambert Field in five below zero weather and headed for the Sunny South.

Our first stop was at Perryville, Missouri, where we visited with some of Klink's friends for several days, and carried nineteen passengers. After leaving Perryville we flew to Hickman, Kentucky, and landed in a soft field east of town. We had passed out of the extremely cold weather and the wheels of our plane sank several inches into the southern mud. When we had refueled and attempted to take-off, it was impossible to get enough speed to lift the tires out of the mud. So Klink got out and I tried to take-off alone. On the third attempt the ship gained enough speed for the wings to begin to carry a portion of the load and keep the wheels from sinking so deeply; then it was only a matter of a few more feet before I was off.

I picked out a hayfield a little further from town, which appeared to be a little more solid than the first, and landed. By that time it was too late to make another hop before dusk, and as even the new field was too soft to make it advisable to carry any passengers, we left the Canuck tied to a fence and went into Hickman for the night.

The first effort to take-off the following morning was unsuccessful, also the second. We could not gain a speed of over five miles an hour over the soft ground. Finally, with the assistance of several men pushing on each wing, we got the ship to the top of a gentle rise which gave us enough of a start to take-off without serious difficulty. We stopped once in Tennessee for fuel; then at Friar Point, Mississippi, where we landed in an old cotton field and tied down for the night.

The Canuck had only one fuel tank with a capacity of twenty-three gallons or enough to last for two and a half hours. By leaving half an hour for locating a landing field, which was quite difficult at times, we had enough gasoline remaining for about one hundred and twenty-five miles in still air. If we were bucking a head wind it would be just that much less.

We spent the night with one of the plantation hands near the field and the next day in seeing the country and carrying a handful of passengers. In the evening we visited a "hanted" house with a party of the younger residents but were unable to find any "hants."

Our next stop was at Hollandale, then Vicksburg, where we landed in a little field six miles north of town by slipping in down the side of a small mountain and ground-looping before striking a stump. After a day seeing Vicksburg we flew to Clinton where the passenger trade was quite lively and another day passed making sightseeing flights.

We refueled at Hattiesburg and Mobile, then landed at the Naval Air Station near Pensacola, Florida, where the Commanding Officer showed us every courtesy during our visit.

At last I received notice from the War Department to the effect that my examination had been satisfactorily passed, along with an order to appear at Brooks Field, San Antonio, Texas, in time to enter the March fifteenth class of Flying Cadets.

Klink and I decided to cut short our stay at Pensacola and to work our way as far west as time would allow before it was necessary for me to leave for Brooks Field.

We had promised to take one of the ladies of the post for a short hop before leaving, and on the

morning of our departure I took off for a test
flight before taking the lady over Pensacola. Just
after the ship had left the field and was about
two hundred feet high over the bay, the motor
"reved" down to about five hundred.   I banked
around in an attempt to get back to the field but
lacked by about fifteen feet enough altitude
to reach it, and was forced to land in the sand
hills less than a hundred feet from the edge
of the flying field.   The first hill wiped off my
landing gear and one wheel went up through the
front spar on the lower left wing, breaking it off
about two feet from the fuselage.

A quick survey of the plane showed that we
would require a new landing gear and propeller
in addition to the material required to splice the
spar.

The Navy hauled the plane into one of its
large dirigible hangars and allowed us to make
use of its equipment in repairing the damage.
We purchased a spare landing gear and a
propeller, then built a box frame around the

broken spar and after gluing all the joints, screwed it in position and wound the splice with strong cord, which was then shrunk tight by several coats of dope. In this way the splice was made stronger than the original spar had ever been.

When we were not working on the ship we made several trips to the old Spanish forts which protected the city during the days when Florida still belonged to Spain. These are in an excellent state of preservation and contain a number of passageways, one of which is supposed to lead underground between the two fortifications, but although we searched carefully for the opening to this tunnel we never found it.

In all we spent about a week repairing the plane and when it was ready to fly once more I tested it with an Irving parachute borrowed from one of the officers of the station. That was the first service type of chute I had ever worn and I experienced the unique feeling of not caring particularly whether the ship held together during the tests or not. I put that Canuck through maneuvers which I would never have dreamed of doing with it before, yet with the confidence of absolute safety.

The advent of the service parachute was a tremendous step forward in the advance of aviation. It gave the test pilot a safe means of escape in most cases when all else had failed. It permitted formations to fly closer in comparative safety and in short allowed flyers to learn more about their planes than ever before. All this contributed to the ever increasing knowledge of practical flying which makes possible the safety of present air commerce.

The airplane parachute has developed with the rapidity of the planes themselves. For years descents with chutes were made from balloons, but the first jump from a plane was by Capt. Berry at St. Louis, Missouri, in 1912. His parachute was a comparatively crude affair and of no use in an emergency. Ten years later, service type parachutes had been perfected which were

strong enough to stand any strain the weight of
a man's body falling through the air could place
on them, no matter how many thousand feet he
fell before releasing the parachute from its pack;
and today, fifteen years after Capt. Berry made
the first jump from an airplane, every army and
air mail pilot is required to wear a parachute.

The test flight over, we lashed a five gallon
can of gasoline on each wing and followed along
the Gulf of Mexico to Pascagoula, Mississippi.
There was a small crack half way down the back
of the Canuck's gasoline tank and when the gas
no longer oozed out through the crack we knew
that the tank was half empty. By carrying the
two gas cans we obtained an extra hour's cruising
range, and when the main tank became low I
would pour their contents into it through a short
length of steam hose. In this way we expected
to make longer flights between landing fields and
partially make up for the time lost at Pensacola.

From Pascagoula we went to New Orleans,
landing in the race track north of the city. Then

to Lake Charles and from there to Rice Field at Houston, Texas. At Rice Field we installed three fuel tanks under the top wing and center section, which gave us twenty-seven gallons extra capacity, or, in addition to the five gallon cans lashed on the wings, a cruising range of about four hundred miles.

The field was covered with water and as our next stop was to be Brooks Field, which is just a few miles south of San Antonio, we only filled the wing and main tanks, leaving the five gallon cans empty.

At Brooks I obtained definite instructions to report not later than March fifteenth.

It was then the end of February but we decided to push on as far west as the intervening time would allow. Then I would return by rail and Klink would continue alone.

We filled all of our tanks and after running along the ground for half a mile, stalled into the air; but after three circles of Brooks Field were completed and the plane was less than fifty feet high we landed and left one of the cans. Klink held the other in his lap in the rear cockpit.

We had no more trouble in attaining several hundred feet of altitude with the lessened load and greatly lessened resistance, which counted for much more than the weight of the gasoline, but an hour later, when the elevation of the ground below us increased as the mountains were approached, we were again just skimming the mesquite and cactus. At last it was necessary for Klink to heave his gas can over the side and for me to turn the ship down a ravine to keep from striking the ground. It was disappointing enough to leave the first can at Brooks Field but I do not believe Klink will ever forget the sight of the second as it burst on the ground below us.

Sometime later we came to the West Nueces River and, mistaking it for the Rio Grande, turned north. We had been cutting across country but had hardly flown long enough to have reached the Rio Grande. The Rio Grande was the only river, according to my map, with a rail-

road running along the northeast bank. We
followed the West Nueces to Camp Wood
where the rails ended. By that time I knew
that the map was in error and we were on the
wrong course, but as there was insufficient
fuel remaining to warrant our cutting across the
mountains to the west, we landed in a small sheep
pasture near Barksdale. This pasture was not
large enough for us both to take off together so
I flew the ship over to Camp Wood alone and
landed in the town square. With the wind blowing from the right direction, and by taking off
under two telephone lines and over one road,
the square afforded a long enough runway, provided the wind was blowing from the proper
direction.

The next day conditions were ideal but Klink
wanted to go to a dance that evening, and the
day after, the wind was blowing from the opposite direction. Our remaining time was passing
rapidly and we were both anxious to get to California before my return to Brooks Field. If we

could get the plane to a larger field six miles south of Camp Wood we would have room to take-off with a full load of gasoline.

One of the town streets was wide enough to take-off from, provided I could get a forty-four foot wing between two telephone poles forty-six feet apart and brush through a few branches on each side of the road later on. We pushed the ship over to the middle of the street and I attempted to take-off. The poles were about fifty feet ahead and just before passing between them there was a rough spot in the street. One of the wheels got in a rut and I missed by three inches of the right wing tip. The pole swung the plane around and the nose crashed through the wall of a hardware store, knocking pots, pans and pitchforks all over the interior.

The merchant and his son thought that an earthquake was in progress and came running out into the street. He was highly pleased to find an airplane halfway into his place of business and not only refused to accept anything for dam-

CURTISS FIELD, L. I.—POLICE GUARDING "THE SPIRIT OF ST. LOUIS," ON ITS WAY TO THE RUNWAY FOR THE TAKE-OFF

CURTISS FIELD, L. I.—CAPTAIN RENÉ FONCK WISHES LINDBERGH THE BEST
OF LUCK

ages, but would not even allow us to have the wall repaired. He said the advertising value was much more than the destruction.

The greatest damage to the plane was a broken propeller, although from that time on it always carried left rudder. We wired for a new propeller and a can of dope from Houston and in a few days were hedgehopping the mountain tops in true Canuck fashion on our way west.

A Canuck, or J.N.4C is nothing more or less than a Canadian Jenny and while it is lighter and performs a little better than a Jenny, it is subject to the same characteristic of being able to just miss most everything it passes over.

We passed over the Rio Grande and cut through a corner of Mexico, then landed on one of the Army emergency fields at Pumpville and induced the section boss to sell us enough gasoline to continue our flight.

Dusk overtook us near Maxon, Texas, and we landed between the cactus and Spanish dagger west of the town, which consisted of a section house and three old box cars of the type used throughout the Southwest for housing the Mexican section hands.

The section boss was living alone. He was soon to be relieved and stationed in some more populated locality. We spent the night with him and in the morning cleared a runway for the ship. Maxon was quite a distance above sea level and as the air was less dense, an airplane required a longer distance to take-off in. There was a small mountain on the east end of the field and the land sloped upwards toward the west. We worked until midday cutting sagebrush and cactus. There was a light breeze from the west and the air was hot and rough. After using three quarters of the runway the Canuck rose about four feet above the ground but stopped there, and when the end of the runway was passed the wings and landing gear scraped along on the sagebrush. As soon as we picked up a little extra flying speed, another clump of sagebrush would slow the ship down again until, after we had gone about two hundred yards, a large Spanish dagger plant passed through the front spar of the lower left wing. After being cut off by the internal brace wires, it remained firmly planted in the center of the outer bay. We landed immediately and found the plane to be undamaged except for a fourteen inch gap in the spar and a number of rips in the wing fabric.

The engineer on a passing freight train had seen us go down and stopped long enough for Klink to climb on board. It was agreed that Klink would go to the nearest place where he could get the material to make repairs, while I remained with the plane. We were thirty-two miles from the nearest store and as the section boss was leaving that day for his new location, I walked a mile and a half to a ranch house, where I arranged for accommodations until we were ready to fly again.

Klink went all the way to El Paso before he could get any dope and wing fabric. Meanwhile

I spent the day with the plane, and a large part of the night following the ranchers' hounds in their search for wildcats and panthers. They had treed a large cat the night before while we were staying in the section house, but were unable to duplicate their performance for my benefit. About all I succeeded in accomplishing after following them for hours, was to pull one dog out of a wire fence which had caught his foot as he jumped over.

Klink returned with a can of pigmented dope, two lengths of crating board, some nails and screws, a can of glue, several balls of chalkline, and enough fabric to replace the torn wing covering. We borrowed a butcher knife, a needle and thread, and an axe from the rancher, and set in to make the Canuck airworthy once more. We hewed the crating down roughly to size, cut it into proper lengths with an old hacksaw blade from our toolkit, and finished it off with the butcher knife. In a short time we had constructed a second box splice similar to the one at

Pensacola, but a few feet farther out on the spar.

We had just enough dope to cover the splice, so the fabric in the outer bay was left undoped; and after we had sewed up the longer rents caused by the sagebrush, we were once more ready to take the air.

It was too near the fifteenth of March to continue west, so we decided to take the Canuck back to San Antonio where we would finish off the repairs and Klink would continue on to California alone.

V

TRAINING AT BROOKS FIELD

I ARRIVED at Brooks Field on March 15th, 1924, but was not enlisted as a Flying Cadet until March 19th. Ordinarily a cadet enlists at the nearest station to his home and is given free transportation to his post of service and back to the enlistment point after his discharge. By enlisting at Brooks I was entitled to no transportation allowance except possibly bus fare back from Kelly where I graduated a year later.

There were one hundred and four of us in all, representing nearly every state in the Union. We filled the cadet barracks to overflowing. There were two cots to each window and some of us were even quartered in the recreation hall.

We were a carefree lot, looking forward to a year of wonderful experiences before we were graduated as second lieutenants and given our wings. Nearly all of us were confident that we would be there to graduate a year later. We had already passed the rigid physical and mental entrance examinations which so many of the other applicants had failed. We had no doubt of our ability to fly although most of us had never flown before, and we had yet to get our first taste of the life of a flying cadet.

By the time we had been in the barracks a few hours stories began circulating around which originated from conversations with the last class of cadets who were waiting to be transferred to the advanced flying school at Kelly.

Rumors of "Benzine Boards" and "wash-outs," "academic work" and "eight-hour examinations," "one eighty's," and "check pilots," "walls with ears" and "cadet etiquette"—these and a hundred other strange terms were condescendingly passed down to us by the old cadets of six months experience. Someone remarked that less than forty per cent of us could expect to finish the primary training at Brooks and that probably half of those would be washed out at Kelly.

By bed check that night we had already begun to feel the apprehension which is a part of a flying cadet's life from his first day at Brooks until he has received his pilot's wings at Kelly.

Our actual flying training was to begin on the first of April. Two weeks were required to become organized and learn the preliminary duties of a cadet. During these two weeks we were inoculated against typhoid and small-pox at the hospital, taught the rudiments of cadet etiquette, given fatigue duty, required to police the grounds surrounding our barracks, inspected daily, and instructed and given examinations in five subjects. In our spare time we were allowed to look around the post or take the bus to San Antonio, provided, however, that we were back in bed not later than ten o'clock on Sunday, Monday, Tuesday, Wednesday, Thursday and

Friday nights. At all other times we could stay out as late as we desired.

When we did have a few spare moments in the afternoon, they were usually spent in trying to "chizzle" a hop from one of the instructors on the line.

Early one morning we were allowed to take the training ships out and push them to the line for the old cadets to fly. But when one of the planes nosed over after eight husky rookies heaved up on the hundred and fifty pound tail, it was decided to put us to work moving hydrogen cylinders for a balloon ascension.

As the first of April approached we were looking forward to the start of actual flying with great anticipation. Coupled with this was the anxiety of waiting for the returns from our examination papers, the failure of any two of which would be sufficient cause for their owner to be washed out from the courses.

The flying instruction was carried on from two stages or different sections of the field. I was assigned to B stage which was about a half mile out in the field from the cadet barracks. Each instructor had about six cadets assigned to him, and early in the morning on the first day of April, our instruction commenced. I was assigned to Sergeant Winston, together with five other cadets. We pushed his instruction plane out from the hangar to the line. Sergeant Winston picked out one of us, told him to get into the rear cockpit and was off. The rest of us walked over to B stage, watching for tarantulas along the road on the way.

In 1924, the Curtiss Jenny was still used by the Army for a training plane, although the 90 H.P. Curtiss OX-5 engines had been replaced by 150 H.P. Hispano-Suizas. The more modern types of planes for training were still in the experimental stage. The Jennies had been designed during the war and they were becoming obsolete, but it is doubtful whether a better training ship will ever be built, although undoubtedly the newest type is much safer. Jennies were underpowered; they were somewhat tricky and they splintered badly when they crashed hard; but when a cadet learned to fly one of them, well, he was just about capable of flying anything on wings with a reasonable degree of safety.

I had been particularly fortunate in my assignment of an instructor. Sergeant Winston held the record for flying time in the army with about thirty-three hundred hours. He was an excellent pilot and knew how to instruct if he wanted to. When my turn came he asked me how much flying time I had had and after I told him about three hundred and twenty-five hours he turned the controls over to me with orders to take the ship around and land it. I had some difficulty in flying with my right hand. The wartime ships which I was accustomed to were built to be flown with the left, but after the Armistice it was decided to change the throttle over to the other side on the theory that the right hand was the natural one to fly with. After three landings, however, Sergeant Winston got out of the cockpit and told me to fly around for thirty minutes and try to get used to right handed piloting.

When we were not flying we were gathered around the stage house watching the progress of our classmates and learning how to turn the propellers over in starting the engine without placing ourselves in a position to be struck in case it kicked backwards. To a pilot, the propeller is the most dangerous part of his plane, and is a constant source of worry to him when his ship is on the ground among people who vie with each other in seeing how close they can stand to the whirring blade while the motor is still running. Then there is usually a contest to see who can be first to move it up and down after it stops turning over.

A cadet is usually given about ten hours of dual instruction before he is allowed to solo. The instructor first takes him up and after flying around for a few minutes, allows the student to take hold of the controls to get an approximate idea of the amount and direction of movement necessary for gentle banks and turns. Then the instructor throws his hands up in the air in full view of the student—the signal that he has turned over entire control of the ship. The cadet is given the opportunity suddenly to realize that flying is not a simple operation of pulling the stick back to go up and pushing it forward to come down, but that an instinctive and synchronized movement of all controls is necessary even to keep the machine in level flight.

For a moment after the pilot turns over the controls the plane keeps on a straight course, then the nose begins to lose its normal position on the horizon, a wing dips down, and a blast of air rushes in from one side of the cockpit. Carefully learned instructions are forgotten and the controls serve only to move the earth still farther from its proper position. All this time the instructor's hands are gripping the top of the cowling. The cadet realizes that it is up to himself in some manner to level the plane out into a normal flying position once more, not realizing for an instant that his instructor can operate the stick nearly as well with his knees as with his hand and that he has probably already saved the plane from falling into a spin several times.

After splashing around the sky in this manner for several minutes the pilot brings his ship back into position and pulling up into a stall with a throttled motor, roars back his instructions at a cadet who is much more absorbed in watching the approaching ground below than in listening to his instructor. When forty-five minutes have passed, the ship is flown back and landed near the stage house where the next cadet, with helmet and goggles adjusted, is waiting for his turn in the air. The first climbs out and takes his place on the bench surrounding the base of the building and the plane is off to repeat the performance over again.

At the end of ten hours, if the cadet is not capable of soloing he is in grave danger of being washed out as a flyer. However, if the instructor believes that a little more time will be sufficient and that the student has shown signs of eventually becoming a military pilot, the dual instruction may be continued for three or four more hours.

At Brooks when an instructor came to the conclusion that one of his students would never master the art of flying quickly enough to keep up with the standard of the class, he turned the cadet over for a check hop with the stage commander who was always a pilot of long experience. Few cadets ever passed this check; if the stage commander believed that any cadet had been misjudged, however, he had authority to place him back on flying status for further instruction. If the commander concurred with the decision of the instructor, he recommended the cadet for a final check on headquarters stage with the chief check pilot. The decision of this officer was final and to be returned to flying after a flight with him was an occurrence seldom recorded in cadet history. After failing his final check flight a cadet was ordered to appear before a board of officers known as the "Benzine Board." If he was reporting for misconduct or academic deficiency there was still some slight hope of beating the board, but if it was for inability to fly, the decision of "washout" was a foregone conclusion.

The washing out for our class commenced in earnest with the approach of solo flights and the returns from our examinations. I was fortunate enough to have passed them and my previous flying experience kept me from worrying on any other account during the first part of our training.

There was no disgrace in washing out. It simply meant in the majority of cases, that the cadet was not especially adapted to flying and he was sent back to his point of enlistment with an honorable discharge and the advice to take up some other form of occupation.

Our first "Benzine Board" met about a month after the start of school and reconvened more or

CURTISS FIELD, L. I.—GETTING READY FOR THE TAKE-OFF. "THE WEATHER WAS PRETTY SICK"

© *Wide World Photos*

CURTISS FIELD, L. I.—JUST BEFORE STARTING ON THE BIG ADVENTURE

less regularly from that time until we were ready to be graduated from the primary school and transferred to Kelly for instructions on service types of planes.

With the washing out process our barracks became less congested. It was not unusual to see the fellows on both sides pack up and cheerfully depart for destinations in different corners of the United States. After a few weeks there would be one bunk standing where eight had been—this in some part of the barracks on which the decisions of the "Benzine Board" had fallen hardest. In another case an entire bay was washed out and left entirely vacant. We never knew who would be next to go, and we could only continue to plug along as best we could with our flying and study a little harder on our ground-school work while we waited for the almost weekly list of washouts to be published on our bulletin board. We were in the full swing of cadet life and under the constant apprehension which accompanies it.

Along with our trials and worries went the fascination of flying together with the priceless goal before us of graduation with an Air Service commission. The wings of the service would be for those of us who were able to survive the rigid training and discipline of a year in the United States Army flying schools.

Always there was something new to look forward to. The start of actual flying; the first solo; learning various stunts and maneuvers; transitions from Jennies to faster and quicker ships; and finally our transfer to Kelly Field, the alma mater of Army fliers.

The Army Air Service was an exacting instructor. There was no favoritism shown and no amount of politics could keep a cadet from being washed out if he fell down in flying. As a result, only a small per cent of those entering Brooks ever graduate from Kelly. In our class of one hundred and four, thirty-three finished their primary training and only eighteen of us received our wings. This appears on the surface to be an unusually low number but as a result of the rigid requirements and careful instruction, our Air Corps schools rank among the best in the world today. They have an extremely low fatality list, not one man in our class being seriously injured.

Probably the most exciting period in our flying training was when the soloing began. The instructor would climb out of his cockpit, tie a white handkerchief on the rudder as a danger signal, indicating that the ship was usually out of control, and signal his student to take off. In some cases the plane would take off nicely, circle the field and make a comparatively good landing. In others the landing would amount to a series of bounces, resulting in the necessity of a second or third attempt before the wheels would hold contact with the ground more than a fraction of a second at a time. In one particular instance, after several futile attempts to get down, the cadet began circling around overhead. His apparent idea was to clinch the chances of landing

on his next attempt by waiting until the gasoline
ran out. His instructor was out in the field trying to flag him down without the slightest success and for half an hour we watched the ship
intently for the first signs of a lowering gas supply; hoping that the fuel would not hold out
much longer as the morning flying period was
nearly over and we were all anxious to see him
land. After half an hour, however, he apparently regained enough courage and determination to make a last attempt at a landing, which
turned out much more successfully than the
others.

When the solo flights were more or less successfully completed the flying instruction was
divided into two periods of forty-five minutes
each. One of these was used for dual and the
other for solo practice.

The instructor would attempt to smooth out
the rough points in his students' flying and demonstrate the method of going through new
maneuvers so that the cadet could be given the

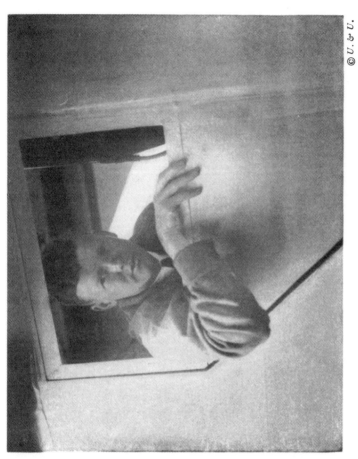

© *U. & U.*

"I DIDN'T USE MY PERISCOPE ALL THE TIME, BUT COULD LOOK OUT MY WINDOWS"

PARIS, FRANCE—A SALUTATION FROM M. BLERIOT

opportunity to go up alone and try out the maneuvers for himself.

One of the first lessons was the "three sixty"— so named because its completion required a total change in direction of three hundred and sixty degrees. The cadet would take off and climb to eight hundred or a thousand feet. The higher he went the less difficulty he had in properly completing the maneuver. Then he would fly into the wind directly over a landing "T" in the center of the field. As the plane passed over the "T" he throttled his motor and made a quick bank either to the right or left depending upon his preliminary instructions. The object was to make a complete circle and land without using the motor, bringing the plane to a stop beside the "T."

"One eightys" were the next requirement and they were probably the cause of more crashes than any other maneuver. They were started in the same manner as the "three sixty," but with the plane heading down wind and at only five hundred feet altitude. They required quick manipulation of controls and a steep bank into the field just before landing.

Next came acrobatics. Loops, spins, barrel rolls, Jenny Immelmans, figure-eights, wingovers, and reversements, every one of which each cadet had to master thoroughly during his course at Brooks.

After the first few weeks had passed we became more or less accustomed to life in the cadet detachment, and found a little time now and then to look around the country and even spend a night in San Antonio. Our examinations were purposely given on Saturday morning so that we would not spend the week end studying. It was well known that too much studying affected a cadet's flying and the school schedule was arranged with that in mind.

Our day began with first call at five forty-five and flying started about seven. At eleven we returned to the barracks and from one to five o'clock was devoted to ground school. After

supper we could study until bed check at ten
o'clock. Plenty of sleep is a necessity for the
student pilot, and that fact is recognized nowhere
more than in the army schools. Every week
night at ten P.M. the cadet officer of the day
checks each bunk and turns in the names of any
vacant ones. Some of our academic subjects,
such as aerodynamics and machine guns required
nearly all of our time after school because of
approaching examinations, whereas others were
comparatively easy and the classroom instruction
was sufficient in itself. When we were not studying there were always plenty of other things to
attract our attention. If one of the boys left the
post, as sometimes happened, he often returned
to find his belongings heaped together in the
middle of the floor with the army cots piled on
top. Several times some cadet returned at midnight to find his equipment carefully transferred
and set up on the roof or in the mess-hall. Another one of the favorite sports was to put a hose
in the bed of a sound sleeper at two A.M. or, if

he slept with his mouth open, to fill it from a tube of shaving cream or hair grease.

One of the fellows found a scorpion in his bed and each night for a week thereafter looked through the bedding for another, but finally became careless and forgot to look. His nearest neighbor promptly placed a number of grasshoppers between the sheets near the foot of the bed.

Another evening it was reported that three pole-cats had crawled into a culvert in front of the barracks. For an hour we attempted to smoke them out. When that failed the fire department was called and we washed them out. The smoke had evidently taken effect, however, and soon three dead pole-cats came floating out from the culvert. The next problem was how to make use of such possibilities. That question was worthy of a most careful consideration. After a survey of the barracks we found that our cadet first sergeant was in San Antonio. There was scarcely one of us who did not have some small score to settle with him so we took one of the pillows from his bed and after removing the pillow case, placed it behind one of the pole-cats. The desired results were then obtained by stepping on the back end of the cat, and after cautiously inserting the pillow back in its case, we replaced it on the first sergeant's bunk. The results were far above expectation. One by one the occupants of that bay arose and carried their cots outside, until by midnight, when our sergeant returned, there were only a half dozen bunks left including his own. By that time the odor had permeated through the other bedding and he was unable to locate the pillow as being the primary cause of offense. Any night for nearly two weeks thereafter our first sergeant and his cot might be located out behind the barracks, and the inspection of quarters, which was to have been held the following morning, was postponed indefinitely.

During our last six weeks at Brooks, life became much less difficult. Most of us who had survived the check pilots and "Benzine Board" were reasonably sure of graduating and although our studies were just as exacting as ever, we were able to absorb them much more easily. Also we had passed our primary flying tests and were making cross country flights in T.W.3's; and learning formation flying in Voughts. And finally we were given a few hours in De Havilands in preparation for the advanced training at Kelly.

We were paired up for the cross country flights. One of us flew on the way out, while the second acted as observer. On the return flight we traded about, so that each achieved an equal amount of experience, both as an observer and as a pilot. These trips were usually laid out in a triangular course, and included landing at each corner of the triangle.

While on one of our first trips from the home airdrome, we landed in the designated field alongside of a road just as a load of watermellons was passing by, so we carried several of them back to the Detachment in our plane.

Always there was some new experience, always something interesting going on to make the time spent in Brooks and Kelly one of the banner years in a pilot's life. The training is rigid and difficult but there is none better. A cadet must be willing to forget all other interest in life when he enters the Texas flying schools and he must enter with the intention of devoting every effort and all of the energy during the next twelve months towards a single goal. But when he receives the wings at Kelly a year later he has the satisfaction of knowing that he has graduated from one of the world's finest flying schools.

VI

RECEIVING A PILOT'S WINGS

IN September, 1924, we were transferred to
Kelly. The time we had looked forward
to for half a year had arrived. We were
through the period of just learning how to fly
and were entering a new experience; that of
learning how to make use of our flying ability
in actual service. We would no longer be floating around the airdrome in machines whose only
purpose was to stand up under the hard knocks
of inexperienced pilots; but we were going to fly
planes which had an actual military value in
warfare.

We were old cadets and felt the importance of
our experience. We were no longer treated as
rookies but as potential officers. Before leaving
Brooks we had conformed with cadet traditions

PARIS, FRANCE—PAUL PAINLEVÉ, FRENCH MINISTER OF WAR, EXTENDS HIS WELCOME. ON THE
RIGHT IS AMBASSADOR MYRON T. HERRICK

PARIS, FRANCE—WITH M. DOUMERQUE AND AMBASSADOR HERRICK

and allowed groups of the new class to gather around us while we gravely spoke of examinations, check pilots, "Benzine Boards," and "washouts." We thoroughly enjoyed the awe inspired by our seventy-five hours of flying experience.

At Kelly our difficulties set in with renewed vigor. The De Havilands did not maneuver like the training Jennies, and we were required to fly as we had never flown before. If a cadet was not able to handle his ship in a maneuver which was at least equal to the standard, he was usually heading towards home within a week.

We were allowed a few days to become accustomed to flying the new type of plane, then an instructor would go up with us to see if our progress had been satisfactory. If so we were sent to the next stage; if not we went up with a check pilot.

From landings we went to the "eight" stage, where were assigned two landmarks such as a tree and a haystack several hundred feet apart, and required to do figure eights around them. Then came the spot landing stage, when we throttled our engine at about a thousand feet and were required to land in a large white circle without using our motor. On this stage we were graded on our take-off, climb, approach, landing, roll, distance from mark, and method of handling the ship. In fact at Kelly we were constantly under observation and our only method of relaxation while flying was when the sky was cloudy and we could get above the clouds.

On one occasion we were flying with a low ceiling and the visibility was not very good. In fact it was an ideal day to do the things we were not supposed to. I was hedgehopping along over the country when I saw another D.H. playing around on my right. I flew over, and after chasing each other around for a while we proceeded to do chandelles, vertical banks, wing overs, and everything else we could think of; all within a few feet of the ground as the clouds themselves were only about three hundred feet high. At last I decided to go up close to the other plane for a little low formation flying, but as I approached I saw that there were two men in the ship and that I had been breaking every rule ever established about low flying with an instructor watching me from another ship. I left that locality with wide open motor and for several days expected to be called on the carpet before the commanding officer on a washout offense. That instructor must have been a good sport, however, because I never heard from him and never was able to find out who he was.

On another occasion, near the end of my course, I came very near being washed out for something I knew nothing about. I had been practicing landings in an S.E.-5 on one corner of Kelly Field. When my time had expired, I landed on the pursuit stage, taxied up to the line, and turned the ship over to the mechanics. That afternoon I was called from class and ordered to report to the operations officer; whereupon he informed me that my flying days were over and that as I knew why, there was no use in explaining further. I was then ordered to report back to my studies.

It came out of a clear sky. I knew of a number of offenses I had committed but none of them at that time. I had actually no idea of what the operations officer was talking about.

When school was over I returned to the operations hut and requested an account of the alleged offense. It appeared that the propeller on my S.E.-5 was cracked, and the spreader-board broken on the landing gear. The crew chief had reported this together with a statement that there were corn stalks hanging on the landing gear, and as there was no corn growing on Kelly Field, that was a sure sign that I had landed away from the airdrome without reporting the fact. A washout offense. We drove to the pursuit stage and found conditions exactly as stated, except that the corn stalks turned out to be weeds, and it was decided that the damage had been caused by a stake left standing in the corner of Kelly

PARIS, FRANCE—CROWDS AT THE CITY HALL AT THE OFFICIAL RECEPTION

PARIS, FRANCE—GUESTS AT THE LUNCHEON OF M. BLERIOT

LEFT TO RIGHT: PAUL PAINLEVÉ CHARLES LINDBERGH, M. BLERIOT, AMBASSADOR HERRICK

Field where I had been landing, although I had not felt the ship strike anything. The cadet who flew the plane earlier in the morning was using the same part of the field and said that he felt it strike a bump on one of his take-offs but did not believe any damage had been done. Who was flying the ship made little difference, however, because as long as he had not landed away from the airdrome without authority, the slight damage was of no consequence. I had come very close to the "Benzine Board" for an offense of which I knew nothing, but it was probably only the open-mindedness and sense of fair play of the operations officer that kept me from being washed out as a result.

One day during the beginning of our term at Kelly, someone decided that the cadets should stand reveille. How it came about or who caused the decision was never known by the detachment, but there was a strong rumor circulated to the effect that our beloved Cadet Sergeant had not forgotten the episode of the pole-

cats. It was an unheard of thing for the cadets
of Kelly to stand formations. We had graduated from that when we left Brooks, and the
thought of continuing it in our advanced status
was, we concluded, degenerating to the morale
of the detachment.

Consequently, when our first sergeant himself
delighted us with verbal visions of being tum-
bled out of bed at first call if we were not up
at the blast of his whistle, we decided that
if it were in the combined power of the detachment, the first call should not sound the next
morning. We could not disobey an order; army
training banishes even the remotest thought of
that; but we might prevent that order from being given. The Cadet Captain and first sergeant were assigned to a private room together.
The rest of us were given cots in the barracks.
While supper was in progress that night the
hands on the sergeant's alarm clock were so
manipulated that the alarm would sound exactly
one hour after the time set. At two o'clock the

next morning a padlock was placed on the hasp outside of his door, and when first call blew a few hours later the cadet detachment slept soundly on.

From spot landings we passed to hurdles. Hurdles require the ship to be brought down without assistance from the engine, and after just passing over a line stretched about eight feet above the ground, to be landed as close as possible to the hurdle. This gave us excellent practice for landing over a fence in a small field.

One of the traditions at Kelly was that anyone knocking down the hurdle must treat the rest to a case of refreshments. It often happened that a pilot was so intent on getting over the hurdle string that he did not notice that his plane was in a stall, and about the time he was over the hurdle the bottom would fall out from under him and his plane would pancake into the ground. Almost every class had one or two minor crack-ups as a result of stalling over the hurdle string.

The De Havilands were not considered safe

for hard stunting and as a result we were only allowed to do wing-overs and split air turns. Diving in excess of one hundred and fifty miles per hour was also forbidden. Consequently only air work allowing us to be thoroughly accustomed to the plane was included in the flying schedule before our formation training began.

The strange field landing training was one of the most interesting parts of our schooling. An instructor would lead a number of planes and land in some field we had never seen before. Then each cadet was required to land and take-off after the instructor. Some of the fields were small and full of obstructions. Yet we had comparatively few even minor crackups. Later each cadet was given an opportunity to lead the rest and pick out a field for them to land in while the instructor trailed.

At Kelly we were given more and longer cross country trips than at Brooks. One of the most important parts of flying training is cross country experience. We made flights to Corpus

Christi, Galveston, Laredo and a number of other places.

Each class spent about two weeks on a gunnery expedition at Ellington Field between Houston and Galveston. Ellington Field was one of the few double fields built during the war, but was later abandoned and, except for a National Guard squadron, was entirely deserted.

We set up our mess in the club house and made the old building which had served as officers' quarters as comfortable as possible. This was in winter and the weather was cold, even in Texas, unusual though it might have been. There were no stoves available so we contrived all sorts of makeshifts to hold a little fire in. If nothing better was obtainable, we shovelled several inches of earth on the floor and devised a hood of some kind leading through a few lengths of tin pipe to the chimney. Of course these fires could not be left unguarded, so it was necessary to put them out in the morning to be rekindled at the close of operations for the day.

Our gunnery work was divided into three parts: ground targets, shadow targets and tow targets. The ground targets were large sheets of paper similar to those used on a rifle range and were set up at an angle on the ground. We shot at these with both the Browning and Lewis machine guns.

The Browning guns on a De Haviland were mounted rigidly in front of the pilot and were synchronized with the engine to shoot between the blades of the propeller. They were capable of firing up to twelve hundred rounds a minute, depending on the motor R.P.M. when they were fired.

Several of us would form a large circle with our planes, and starting our dive from about one thousand feet, would fire short bursts into the target on the ground. After completing our bursts we would zoom back up into the circle while the next ship started its dive. Each plane had its individual target.

After emptying the Browning guns we gave

our observers a chance with their Lewises by circling low around the targets. On the next flight the pilot and observer traded places.

The Lewis gun is mounted on a turret on the rear cockpit. Two guns were usually used together and they could be pointed in any direction.

After a few days on ground targets we were sent out over Trinity Bay for shadow targets. One plane is flown fairly high over the water while another fires at its shadow. The splashes from the bullets are easily seen and the accuracy of marksmanship very apparent.

The tow targets are by far the most difficult of the three varieties, and require skillful maneuvering and excellent marksmanship. They consist of a cloth sleeve similar to a wind sock which is towed a few hundred feet behind a De Haviland flying at sixty or sixty-five miles an hour.

When the forward or Browning guns were used, the attacking ship approached the tow target head on, firing one or two short bursts as it passed. In this way there was no danger of the occupants of the towing plane being struck by a wild shot. The De Havilands were much too large to use the forward guns effectively on a tow target. Any accurate shooting required the quick maneuverability of a pursuit ship.

The Lewis guns were used while flying parallel with the target and were very effective. When we were close enough we could often see the tracers pass directly through the cloth sleeve.

After returning from Ellington Field we were given a few hours in each of the various types of service airplanes. The M.B.-3 and the S.E.-5 scouts; the Martin Bombers with their twin Liberty engines; the T.W.-5 two-place transition planes; and the little Sperry messengers. In this way we obtained experience in each branch: pursuit, attack, observation and bombardment. Later we were given our choice of which we desired to specialize in. If our wishes corresponded with the judgment of the instructors we were assigned to that branch.

Together with three other cadets and four student officers, I was sent to the pursuit stage, where we spent the few remaining weeks of our course, piloting the S.E.-5 and the M.B.-3 single seaters.

Pursuit combines a little of every branch of the air corps. In addition to formation combat, dog fighting, and ground straffing, the pursuit pilot is often called upon to make observations and do light bombing.

A great deal of our time was devoted to formation flying. Air combat of the future will probably often be between large formations rather than individual pilots, and it is accordingly of utmost importance for the pursuit pilot to hold his place in formation instinctively, so that his entire attention can be devoted to the enemy rather than to his own formation.

We often maneuvered our flights while the individual planes were less than ten feet apart and it was not unusual to dive vertically for several thousand feet in a fairly close formation.

We learned the use of Lufbery circles, cross over turns, and other formation tactics. Our formations were often tight, it is true, but strange as it may seem, very few accidents occur from too close flying. A pilot is constantly alert when his plane is only a short distance from the one in front and nothing is allowed to distract his attention. On the other hand, when there is quite some distance separating them he is often more engrossed in lighting a cigarette or watching some object on the ground than in his own formation.

In pursuit flying we came to have great confidence in our parachutes. The planes we were flying were kept in excellent condition and none ever failed, notwithstanding the fact that we placed them under every conceivable strain imaginable. But the knowledge that we did not have to concern ourselves about whether they did fall apart or not was an invaluable factor in building up our morale. Our formations were tighter, the combats faster, and our flying better as a result.

We had a number of close calls but considering the amount of flying we had done, and that all of it was military flying, which cannot be ever compared to commercial traffic as far as safety is concerned, our accidents were remarkably few and none resulted seriously.

No one knows of the risk he takes better than the pursuit pilot and no one is less concerned about it. Every move, although at lightning speed, is made with a coolness born of experience and love of flying. The army Air Corps is built up of men who fly for the love of flying. Their only mission in life is to build up the finest air corps in the world, and their greatest desire is to be given the opportunity to do so without restriction. If an officer is lost in duty he would be the last one to wish for resulting restrictions on his comrades.

A week of our pursuit training was spent on a gunnery expedition at Galveston. We flew

there from Kelly Field in M.B.3A. machines
and fired on tow targets exclusively. Our field
was close to the Gulf, and when the day's operations had been completed we were free to go
about as we chose. Consequently a large part of
the evening was spent along the rocky beach.

On the night of our last day at Galveston several of us were holding a contest to decide which
could reach the most distant rock between the
breakers, before the next wave rolled in. One of
the fellows was outstanding in his accomplish-
ments. In fact he was so dextrous that none of
us could compete, so we were all loud in our
praises and unanimously agreed that there was
not a rock in the gulf too obscure for him. There
was, however, a rock a number of feet beyond the
most distant point any of us had attained, which
was visible only for an instant as the last breaker
receded and before the next arrived. Even this
was possible, we confidently assured him.

He watched that rock intently for several
minutes; then bolstered up by our praise and

his own confidence, he stood poised and ready. At the proper moment he nimbly leaped from boulder to boulder after the retreating surf but just before the final rock was touched a large wave towered above it. Too late! The chance of retreat had never been considered and its opportunity had passed. With do or die determination he leaped onto the boulder and into the breaking wave. This incident would not have been serious or its consequences important had we been able to carry any extra equipment in our pursuit planes, but as it was, extra clothing was a scarce article, and when we took off for San Antonio and Kelly the following morning, it was necessary for him to send his wet clothes back in a De Haviland and make his flight in a bearskin flying suit without insulation against the bearskin.

In warm weather these suits acquired an odor similar to that of a goat which has been in the barn all winter and the fur itself was far from comfortable. On the trip back a piston froze in the engine. For two days the cadet was alternately roasting in the southern sun and freezing in the Texas nights while he guarded his ship and waited for a new engine.

After our return from Galveston while we were practicing formation attack on two seaters, I experienced one of the incidents of the military pilot's life. I made my first emergency parachute jump. When an Army plane crashes, the pilot is required to write a detailed report of the crash. My account was as follows:

"A nine-ship SE-5 formation, commanded by Lieut. Blackburn, was attacking a DH4B, flown by Lieut. Maughan at about a 5,000 foot altitude and several hundred feet above the clouds. I was flying on the left of the top unit, Lieut. McAllister on my right, and Cadet Love leading. When we nosed down on the DH, I attacked from the left and Lieut. McAllister from the right. After Cadet Love pulled up, I continued to dive on the DH for a short time before pulling up to the left. I saw no other ship nearby.

I passed above the DH and a moment later felt a slight jolt followed by a crash. My head was thrown forward against the cowling and my plane seemed to turn around and hang nearly motionless for an instant. I closed the throttle and saw an SE-5 with Lieut. McAllister in the cockpit, a few feet on my left. He was apparently unhurt and getting ready to jump.

"Our ships were locked together with the fuselages approximately parallel. My right wing was damaged and had folded back slightly, covering the forward right-hand corner of the cockpit. Then the ships started to mill around and the wires began whistling. The right wing commenced vibrating and striking my head at the bottom of each oscillation. I removed the rubber band safetying the belt, unbuckled it, climbed out past the trailing edge of the damaged wing, and with my feet on the cowling on the right side of the cockpit, which was then in a nearly vertical position, I jumped backwards as far from the ship as possible. I had no difficulty in

locating the pull-ring and experienced no sensation of falling. The wreckage was falling nearly
straight down and for some time I fell in line
with its path and only slightly to one side. Fear-
ing the wreckage might fall on me, I did not pull
the rip cord until I dropped several hundred feet
and into the clouds. During this time I had
turned one-half revolution and was falling flat
and face downward. The parachute functioned
perfectly; almost as soon as I pulled the rip
cord the riser jerked on my shoulders, the leg
straps tightened, my head went down, and the
chute fully opened.

"I saw Lieut. McAllister floating above me
and the wrecked ships pass about 100 yards to
one side, continuing to spin to the right and leaving a trail of lighter fragments along their path.
I watched them until, still locked together, they
crashed in the mesquite about 2000 feet below
and burst into flames several seconds after
impact.

"Next I turned my attention to locating a

PARIS, FRANCE—WITH AMBASSADOR HERRICK ON THE STEPS OF THE EMBASSY, JUST AFTER
ARRIVAL IN PARIS

LONDON, ENGLAND—THE WELCOME AT CROYDEN FIELD WHERE A MILLING MOB OF NEARLY HALF A MILLION HAD GATHERED

landing place. I was over mesquite and drifting in the general direction of a plowed field which I reached by slipping the chute. Shortly before striking the ground, I was drifting backwards, but was able to swing around in the harness just as I landed on the side of a ditch less than 100 feet from the edge of the mesquite. Although the impact of landing was too great for me to remain standing, I was not injured in any way. The parachute was still held open by the wind and did not collapse until I pulled in one group of shroud lines.

"During my descent I lost my goggles, a vest pocket camera which fitted tightly in my hip pocket, and the rip cord of the parachute."

During the descent all the other planes broke formation and arched around us. Every ship within sight proceeded at full speed to the spot and before long the air was full of machines. Several of the De Havilands landed in the plowing and within half an hour two planes with extra parachutes were sent to take us back to

Kelly. About an hour after the crash we had two new S.E.-5's and were back in the air again.

The parachute is a marvelous invention, experimented with as early as the 16th century by Leonardo da Vinci.

The first parachute was built by a Frenchman in 1784. This parachute was a rigid structure covered with very strong paper and fabric. It was used in a jump from a building in Paris.

About a year later the same type of parachute was dropped from a hot air balloon in England. Soon jumps began to be made from balloons with other types of rigid parachutes.

About 1880, Captain Thomas Baldwin made a name for himself by jumping from hot-air balloons with a chute which was a forerunner of the present type. He was the first really successful jumper, but success in those days was judged by how long a man lived in this profession.

In 1912, the first parachute jump from an airplane was made. ·The container was attached to the plane and the man who did the jumping pulled the parachute out as he fell.

The war really proved that the parachute is a life saving apparatus for use with airplanes. Early in 1918 the allied pilots reported that German pilots were using parachutes to escape from their planes whenever they were out of control or set on fire. This was the beginning of insistent demands on the part of our allied pilots for parachute equipment. The A.E.F. tried to produce a satisfactory parachute by combining the good feature of several chutes already in existence. All of these, however, were very bulky and heavy and hard to get on the plane.

During the summer of 1918, the U. S. Air Service officials appealed to Washington for good airplane parachutes. A large number of tests were made. Finally, after combining all the good points of foreign and American chutes, a satisfactory free type of parachute was developed. By free type I mean the kind of parachute which is entirely independent of the plane.

Stories often come out in the newspapers about parachutes that fail to open. What probably really happens is that men who make jumps from planes are killed before they are able to pull the rip cord which opens the parachute. In the past there was always a great deal of danger in testing out a new type of chute, but now they have been developed to such a high degree of efficiency that there are practically no fatalities. Each parachute that is used by the government is repacked every month and tested every six months.

Altogether, about 57 lives have been saved by parachutes in government service. In every instance the jump took place because of fog, engine failure while flying over unfavorable country, collision of planes or other very definite emergencies. They say in the service that any flyer who jumps to save his life becomes a member of the "Caterpillar Club." This is because the parachute is made entirely of silk, and silk comes from caterpillars. All the 57 members of this club feel that their lives have been saved by the silkworm caterpillar!

There is a saying in the service about the parachute: "If you need it and haven't got it, you'll never need it again!" That just about sums up its value to aviation.

For two of the last days we were on tactical maneuvers with the other branches. Half of our number were assigned to defend the bombers and observation planes while the other half attacked them. When we met, a lively combat ensued and the air would be full of pursuit planes in every conceivable position, each trying to get on the tail of an enemy plane without being first shot down itself.

At night in the barracks we would argue about which side won the war, but whenever one of us would demonstrate to the enemy that he had been shot down in battle, another would interpose the claim that he had put the attacking ship out of commission several minutes previous to the combat.

When graduation day arrived eighteen of us remained of the hundred and four cadets who started the course at Brooks a year before. We were presented with our wings and commissioned second lieutenants in the Air Service Reserve Corps. That night we gave a farewell dinner in San Antonio and for the last time assembled together.

The next day we departed from Kelly.

VII

I WENT by rail to St. Louis and took an O.X.-5 Standard out for a barnstorming trip in Illinois, Missouri and Iowa. The Post Office Department had just advertised a number of contract air mail routes for bid, one of which was between St. Louis and Chicago by way of Springfield, Ill. I decided to barnstorm around the country until it was determined which bidder would be assigned the contract. The Robertson Aircraft Corp. had placed a bid and offered me the position of chief pilot if they were successful in getting the contract.

After returning from Iowa I flew on several flying circus dates and made a few short cross country flights to nearby cities.

On June second, while testing a commercial plane built at Lambert Field, I was forced to make a second emergency jump. I had flown the ship for a few minutes the previous week and on this occasion was testing it for various maneuvers. I had completed everything except tailspins, but when I attempted a right spin the plane refused even to start, so after a second attempt with the same result I gave that up and tried one to the left. The ship fell in easily and, when I reversed the controls after a half turn, came out at once. I then put it into a second left spin and held the controls in a spinning position during two complete turns. When I reversed them they had no apparent effect and using the engine was of no assistance. After trying for fifteen hundred feet to bring the ship out of the spin, I rolled over the right side of the cockpit and, since I had jumped only about three hundred and fifty feet above the ground, I pulled the rip cord as soon as the stabilizer had passed. The chute opened quickly but while it was functioning, I had fallen faster than the spinning ship. On its next revolution the plane was headed directly towards the chute. How close it passed will never be known, for the risers leading up from my harness were twisted and swung me around as the ship passed. However, less than twenty-five feet intervened between the wing and my parachute.

I watched the plane crash in a grainfield and turned my attention to landing. A strong wind was drifting me towards a row of high tension poles and it was necessary to partially collapse the chute in order to hasten the descent and land before striking the wires. I landed rather solidly in a potato patch and was dragged several feet and over a road before several men arrived and collapsed the chute. In addition to the strong wind and rough air, collapsing or "cutting" the chute so close to the ground had caused a very rapid descent, and my shoulder had been dislocated in landing.

In July I went on two weeks active duty at

Richards Field, Missouri, where I instructed on Jennies and D.H.-4's. In August I flew a Curtiss Oriole to Nevada, Missouri, to carry passengers during the Missouri National Guard encampment.

While at Nevada I received a proposition to fly in a circus in Colorado and, as there was no immediate prospect of starting work on the mail route, I accepted and when the encampment ended I flew the Oriole back to St. Louis and took a train west.

On arriving at the field a few miles east of Denver, I discovered the plane I was to fly to be the same Lincoln Standard that Lynch and I had flown to Montana three years before. We did a little barnstorming along the eastern slope of the Rockies preliminary to the start of our flying circus. We had contracted to exhibit before a number of fairs in Colorado and there was nothing barred in the exhibitions. We put on everything the committee was willing to pay for. At the smaller places we used only one plane, but at the more important exhibitions two were required.

We flew to the town where a fair was taking place about one day before we were to exhibit. In that way everything was in readiness for the circus and the next morning there was no delay in our performance.

We started with wing-walking. The performer would climb out of the cockpit and walk along the entering edge of the wing to the outer bay strut, where he climbed up onto the top wing, and stood on his head as we passed the grandstand. After finishing his stunts on the wing he would go to the landing gear and from there to the center section, where he sat while the plane looped and did Jenny Immelmans. From the center section he went to the tail and then, unless it was an unusual occasion, the wing-walking exhibition was over.

After wing-walking came the breakaway. This was accomplished by fastening a cable to the landing gear. The performer went out to the wingtip, fastened his harness to the loose end of the cable and to all appearances fell off the wing. No one on the ground could see the cable and a breakaway always produced quite a sensation. Iron loops were clamped along the cable for use in climbing back up.

One of our feature attractions was the plane change. A rope ladder was attached to the wing of a plane and as one ship flew past the grandstand with the performer standing near the tip of the top wing, a second plane with the ladder attached, passed over the first, so that the ladder was in easy reach of the performer. We usually made two fake attempts to effect the change and actually counted on the third for success. In this way the feat looked more difficult.

A parachute was attached to the opposite wing from the rope ladder. After the plane change was completed, the performer jumped off with the chute and the show was over.

In the evening we made a night fireworks flight. A series of candles, which when lighted

emitted a trail of fire for several hundred feet behind the ship, was attached to each wing. After
these candles had burned out, two magnesium
flares started burning, lighting up the country
below well enough to read a book very clearly.
The display was set off by an electric battery in
the cockpit.

When the plane reached an altitude of two or
three thousand feet, a number of bombs were
dropped to attract attention; then the switch was
thrown in to start the trails and colored lights,
and the ship looped and shunted around the
comet-like trail of fire.

Our greatest difficulty in night flying lay in
lighting the landing fields from which to operate.
Sometimes a number of cars were on the field
and I landed and took off across the beams of
their headlights.   Under such conditions the
ground was well illuminated and landing very
simple.   On other occasions there would not be
more than one car available and in one instance,
on a dark night, I took off and landed by the

light of a pocket flashlight which one of the men flashed constantly while I was in the air, to enable me to keep track of the landing field.

At one town in Colorado, we were booked for a fireworks exhibition to be given between darkness and midnight. We had been barnstorming during the day and on our way to this town we ran short of lubricating oil. By the time we had replenished our supply it was too late to get in before dark, and I had never landed at that town before. The owner of the plane, however, was sure that he could easily locate the landing field, even in darkness. He had been there many times and he knew that the field was "right next to the golf links."

We arrived over the town and after circling a few times, I throttled the motor and shouted "Where's the field?"

The reply was immediate and full of confidence, "Right next the golf links."

"Well, where are the golf links?"

"I don't know!"

I was up against another of the very amusing
but equally serious incidents in barnstorming life.
We were over strange territory on a dark night
and with a rapidly diminishing fuel supply. It
was imperative to land within a very few
minutes, yet it was not possible to tell one field
from another, and even the line fences were not
visible.

I flew around until the outline of a strawstack
appeared in the field below us. This field was
outlined on one side by the lighter color of the
pasture adjoining it and a number of trees were
discernible along the end. There was no way
of telling whether it contained posts or ditches,
but we had no alternative, and I landed beside
the strawstack in the center.

A hasty examination of the field showed it to
be suitable for night flying and we hailed the first
car passing for a ride into the town. We had
difficulty in locating our fireworks and, as the
stores were all closed, still more time was lost
before we obtained the bailwire, nails and boards

used in building the framework for the flares and candles and attaching it to the plane.

It was nearly midnight when the ship was at last ready for the display. Only one car remained on the field. We ran this machine out beside the strawstack and placed it in a position to show up on one side of the stack, in addition to throwing most of its light on the field. I was about to take-off when the headlights on the car became so dim that they were entirely useless. One of the men had a pocket flashlight and I took-off while he threw its beam on the strawstack.

It was eleven-forty when I left the ground and eleven-fifty seven when the last flare had burned out. Our contract had been fulfilled with three minutes to spare.

I located the field by the flashing of the spotlight and levelled off and landed by its beam.

If the position of a light is known and the field is fairly level, it is not necessary to see the ground, but a plane can be stalled in and landed on the darkest night. Pilots often bring their ships

BRUSSELS, BELGIUM—WITH CROWN PRINCE LEOPOLD DURING THE
OFFICIAL RECEPTION

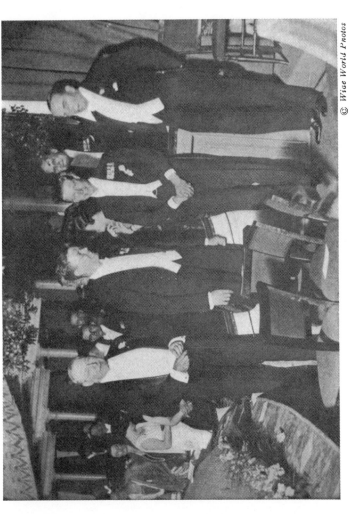

LONDON, ENGLAND—WITH H. R. H. THE PRINCE OF WALES AND LORD LONSDALE (LEFT) IN THE ROYAL BOX AT THE DERBY BALL

down when only the outline of a field is visible. For this reason it is imperative that no obstructions such as farm machinery, or live stock, be allowed to remain on a landing field at night.

Locating a strange flying field by its position in relation to an equally strange golf course, is just one of the many instances in a pilot's life where comedy goes hand in hand with the most serious situations.

In one instance, the story is told of a young pilot who had just learned to fly. He was taking the owner of his plane for a short flight and was demonstrating the various maneuvers he had learned. Finally he put the machine into a spin, but after several turns, discovered that he was not able to come out, and after trying vainly in every way he could remember hearing of from his instructor, he leaned forward in the cockpit and tensely informed his passenger that they were about to crash. Not realizing the seriousness of the situation, the owner replied, "What the —— do you care, it's not your ship!"

It was usually the case that a person inexperienced in the art of flying became quite disturbed over some trivial thing that was of little importance, yet was perfectly at home and enjoying life tremendously at a time when the pilot was straining every effort to avoid disaster.

People would argue indefinitely, trying to persuade one of us to overload the plane past its danger point by carrying more than two passengers at a time from a small field, and it was of no consequence to them whether the plane cleared the nearest trees by a safe margin, or stalled over the uppermost branches by inches. Explanations on our part were next to useless.

If we refused to overload the ship someone cited an example where a plane had carried several passengers at one time and it made no difference what kind of a machine it was, or how large an airport it was operating from. The fact that it carried more passengers than we did indicated that it was operated by a better

pilot, and that our plane was not as safe to ride
in.

We could struggle along close to the ground
trying to get a little altitude and our passengers
would have the time of their lives, waving at the
people below, but let the motor start to miss, although the plane might be several thousand feet
high, with several large fields in sight, and they
would glance nervously back at the pilot wishing
that they had never considered taking a ride in
an airplane.

The International Air Races were to be held,
that year, at New York during the first part of
October and, since our fair contracts were over
by the last of September, we decided to enter in
the "On to New York" competition, which was
for civilian planes only, and was decided by
points given for distance, speed, number of passengers carried, and the size of the engine used.

We had our motor overhauled at Denver and
expected to fly from there to San Francisco for
the start. Some of the repair parts for the en-

gine were delayed and we were several days late in leaving Denver. Even then it was only through night work and leaving a number of things undone that we got away. A fifty-gallon center section gasoline tank had been installed which, in addition to the regular fuselage tank, gave us a capacity of one hundred and seven gallons.

We installed the engine one night and idled it for several hours before daybreak in order to work in the bearings; then we took off for San Francisco.

Our first stop was at Rawlins, Wyoming, where the highest field on the transcontinental air mail route is located. We refilled at Rawlins and made Evanston that night.

At Evanston we were starting the engine preparatory to taxi-ing over and tying down for the night, when our carburetor caught fire. In the haste to get started we had neither put a fire screen on the intake, nor a drain pipe down from the bowl. The engine was covered with oil and the gasoline overflowing from the bowl carried the flames down around it. Soon the entire nose of the ship was ablaze and although we shovelled earth over the motor, it appeared that the wings would soon catch fire. If the fabric began to burn, the ship was gone. I had just finished removing all loose equipment from the cockpit when a small hand extinguisher arrived and with its aid the fire was soon put out.

All of the ignition wire insulation was burned off but otherwise very little damage had been done.

We were delayed twenty-four hours rewiring the engine and cleaning out the dirt shovelled on in the attempt to put out the fire.

After Rawlins we stopped at Salt Lake City, and from there we flew over the Great Salt Lake Desert to Battle Mountain, Nevada, where we spent the night.

We took off from Battle Mountain with full gas tanks and after following the passes until part of the fuel was consumed, and the load cor-

respondingly lightened, we passed over the Sierra
Nevada Range at eight thousand five hundred
feet, and landed at Oakland, California. The
same evening, without refilling, we flew over San
Francisco Bay to Crissey Field.

The following day we took off from Crissey
Field on the start of our race to New York. One
of the rules of the contest was that each plane
should carry a log with the starting point and
number of passengers carried attested to by two
witnesses. By the time we had made out the
log and serviced our plane, it was afternoon and
darkness overtook us at Lovelocks, Nevada.

The next night was spent in Rawlins, Wyoming, after a stop at Salt Lake City for fuel.

We arrived in Rawlins with a valve blowing
badly and were delayed a day in pulling the
bank and grinding in another valve.

We were far behind our schedule due to the
late start from Denver; the delay at Evanston,
and again at Rawlins; but without further
trouble we would still be able to reach New

York on time. Another valve began blowing,
however, soon after leaving Rawlins, and when
we took-off from our next stop at Sidney,
Nebraska, the motor had lost a number of revo-
lutions.

We flew to Lincoln from Sidney and after
taking the short remaining time into consideration, we decided to abandon the race and start
barnstorming.

We overhauled the engine at Lincoln and
worked over towards St. Louis, where we arrived
about the end of October.

At St. Louis we decided to tie up for the
winter and I began instructing students for
the Robertson Aircraft Corporation on OX-5
Standards. The Corporation had been awarded
the air mail contract but actual operation was
not to start until the next spring, so during
the winter months I spent my time instructing
and test flying in their commercial service.

For the first time in my flying career I was
to be in one place longer than a few months, so

in November, 1925, I enlisted in the 110th Observation Squadron of the 35th Division Missouri National Guard, and was commissioned a First Lieutenant soon afterward.

The squadron was stationed on Lambert Field. Every Sunday was spent in flying. We had a number of J.N. training planes and one T.W.-3 which was the commanding officer's personal ship.

The organization was composed mainly of pilots who had flown during the war, but after the Armistice had gone back to civilian life. Their only method of keeping in training was by flying National Guard planes in their spare moments and attending camp two weeks each year.

Two nights and one day each week were devoted to military service by these officers and the enlisted men under them. Their pay was small and most of them lost more from neglect of their business than they received for their military services. The remuneration was hardly considered. However they joined the Guard for two reasons: first, because of the opportunity it offered to keep in flying training, and second, because they considered it a patriotic duty to keep fit for immediate service in case of National emergency.

Appropriations were not large and often insufficient but, although at times it required part of the squadron's pay checks, the ships were kept in the air.

The National Guard squadrons offer an excellent opportunity for young men to get a start in aviation. Instruction is given each week, covering practically every branch of military aeronautics, and practical flying experience is obtained both in the air and on the ground under actual operating conditions. Each year a few members of the squadron are sent to the army schools at San Antonio for flying training, and upon returning these men take their places in the commissioned personnel of the organization.

The inauguration of our Air Mail service was to take place on April fifteenth, and as spring drew near we were kept busy making preliminary preparations. The De Havilands were to be completed and tested; a ground organization built up; the terminal airports decided upon and facilities for taking on and discharging the mail arranged for; in addition to the untold detail arrangements which go to make up the organization of a successful airline.

Contract air mail routes are located by the Post Office Department and are so arranged that the mail service can be improved by use of air transportation over other means of communication.

The route is opened for bid and the contract awarded to the lowest bidder who is responsible and in a position successfully to carry on operations.

The contractor can bid any amount up to three dollars per pound of mail and is paid by the pound for the actual amount carried over his route.

Our route, between St. Louis and Chicago was

operated on a schedule which saved one business day over train service to New York. A letter mailed in St. Louis before three-thirty P.M. was rushed to Lambert Field by a fast mail truck, transferred to the plane which was waiting with engine turning over, landed on the Air Mail field at Maywood, Illinois at seven-fifteen, transferred to one of the Chicago-New York overnight planes, retransferred at Cleveland, Ohio, and was in the Post Office in New York in time for the first morning delivery.

An answer could be mailed at New York in the evening and be delivered in St. Louis before noon on the following day. If sent through the ordinary mail it would not arrive until one day later.

The advantages of air transportation are most apparent over long distances. The air mail flies from New York to San Francisco in thirty-six hours, whereas a train requires nearly four days to make the same trip.

The United States, through the efforts of the

Post Office and the Department of Commerce, is being covered with a network of air mail routes, and it is only a matter of the public using this service before nearly every city in the country will be served by airlines.

VIII

TWO EMERGENCY JUMPS

BY the first of April our organization was
well under way and about a week before
the inauguration day we took two planes
over the route to make any final arrangements
necessary.

On April fifteenth at 5:50 A.M. I took-off
from the Air Mail Field at Maywood on the first
southbound flight, and that afternoon we sent two
ships north with the inauguration mail from St.
Louis, Springfield and Peoria.

During the summer months most of our route
was covered during daylight, but as winter approached the hours of night flying increased
until darkness set in a few minutes after we left
the field at St. Louis.

With night flying and bad weather our troubles

began. Our route was not lighted at first and the intermediate airports were small and often in poor condition. Our weather reports were unreliable and we developed the policy of taking off with the mail whenever local weather conditions permitted. We went as far as we could and if the visibility became too bad we landed and entrained the mail.

One of the worst conditions we met with was in flying from daylight into darkness. It was not difficult to fly along with a hundred foot ceiling in the daytime, but to do so at night was an entirely different matter, and after the night set in, if the weather became worse, it was not possible to turn around and return to daylight.

With all of our difficulties, however, the mail went through with surprising regularity. During the first five months of operation we made connections on over ninety-eight per cent of our trips.

There are only two conditions which delay the air mail: fog and sleet. If the fog is light or local, and the sleet not too heavy, the planes continue even then.   But when the ground becomes invisible and the fog covers the terminal fields, or when sleet freezes thickly on wings and wires, the planes cannot continue.   In such cases the mail is entrained and usually reaches its destination at least as soon as it would have if sent by train in the first place.

Almost every day, in some section of the United States, mail pilots are flying over fog and through storms and rain to bring their ships through on schedule time.   The mail plane is seldom delayed and then only by impossible weather conditions.   In the future these delays will become fewer as radio navigation and instruments for blind flying improve, until it will be possible for the pilots to keep to their schedules under the worst conditions and in comparative safety.

Another hazard, during certain times of year, is the formation of ice.   This will gather on all parts of the plane but mainly on the wires, propeller, and entering edge of the wings.   If it forms slowly from a fog or light rain, a plane may be able to continue on its course for some time, but if a heavy sleet storm is encountered the ice may form so rapidly that a ship cannot stay in the air over five minutes before it is so loaded down that the pilot will be unable to keep from losing altitude even with his motor wide open.

The actual weight of ice is not as important as the loss in efficiency of the wing, due to the changed airfoil caused by ice gathering on the entering edge.

Still more loss is caused from the ice forming on the propeller itself. The blades take on a thick coating which continues to increase in depth until the ice from one of the blades is thrown off by centrifugal force. When this happens an excessive vibration sets in and continues until ihe opposite blade has thrown off its coating.

One of the dangers which a mail pilot faces in flying at night through bad weather and low

LONDON, ENGLAND—CROWDS PRESSING AROUND "THE SPIRIT OF ST. LOUIS" AS THE PLANE LANDED. SOME OF THE SOUVENIR-HUNTERS MANAGED TO TEAR AWAY BITS OF THE WING

© *Wide World Photos*

LONDON, ENGLAND—"AT CROYDEN FIELD I ESCAPED TO THE TOP OF THE
OBSERVATION TOWER OVERLOOKING THE CROWD"

visibility is in suddenly losing track of the ground due to a fog bank lower than the rest. If he has been flying very close to the ground it is not advisable to go lower, and often the only alternative is to climb up through the fog and attempt to find a hole somewhere to spiral down through.

Being caught in a fog at night was the cause of two of my forced jumps, the official reports of which follow:

"I took off from Lambert-St. Louis Field at 4:25 P.M., September 16, 1926, and after an uneventful trip arrived at Springfield, Ill., at 5:10 P.M., and Peoria, Ill., at 5:55 P.M.

"I left the Peoria Field at 6:10 P.M. There was a light ground haze, but the sky was practically clear with but scattered cumulus clouds. Darkness was encountered about 25 miles northeast of Peoria, and I took up a compass course, checking on the lights of the towns below until a low fog rolled in under me a few miles northeast of Marseilles and the Illinois River.

"The fog extended from the ground up to about 600 feet, and, as I was unable to fly under it, I turned back and attempted to drop a flare and land. The flare did not function and I again headed for Maywood (Chicago's air mail port) hoping to find a break in the fog over the field. Examination disclosed that the cause of the flare failure was the short length of the release lever and that the flare might still be used by pulling out the release cable.

"I continued on a compass course of 50 degrees until 7:15 P.M. when I saw a dull glow on top of the fog, indicating a town below. There were several of these light patches on the fog, visible only when looking away from the moon, and I knew them to be towns bordering Maywood. At no time, however, was I able to locate the exact position of the field, although I understand that the searchlights were directed upward and two barrels of gasoline burned in an endeavor to attract my attention. Several times I descended to the top of the fog, which was 800

to 900 feet high, according to my altimeter.
The sky above was clear with the exception of
scattered clouds, and the moon and stars were
shining brightly. After circling around for 35
minutes I headed west to be sure of clearing
Lake Michigan, and in an attempt to pick up
one of the lights on the Transcontinental.

"After flying west for fifteen minutes and seeing no break I turned southwest hoping to strike
the edge of the fog south of the Illinois River.
My engine stopped at 8:20 P.M., and I cut in the
reserve. I was at that time only 1,500 feet high,
and as the engine did not pick up as soon as I
expected I shoved the flashlight in my belt and
was about to release the parachute flare and
jump when the engine finally took hold again.
A second trial showed the main tank to be dry,
and accordingly a maximum of twenty minutes'
flying time left.

"There were no openings in the fog and I decided to leave the ship as soon as the reserve tank
was exhausted. I tried to get the mail pit open

with the idea of throwing out the mail sacks, and then jumping, but was unable to open the front buckle. I knew that the risk of fire with no gasoline in the tanks was very slight and began to climb for altitude when I saw a light on the ground for several seconds. This was the first light I had seen for nearly two hours, and as almost enough gasoline for fifteen minutes' flying remained in the reserve, I glided down to 1,200 feet and pulled out the flare release cable as nearly as I could judge over the spot where the light had appeared. This time the flare functioned but only to illuminate the top of a solid bank of fog, into which it soon disappeared without showing any trace of the ground.

"Seven minutes' gasoline remained in the gravity tank. Seeing the glow of a town through the fog I turned towards open country and nosed the plane up. At 5,000 feet the engine sputtered and died. I stepped up on the cowling and out over the right side of the cockpit, pulling the rip cord after about a 100-foot fall. The

parachute, an Irving seat service type, functioned perfectly; I was falling head downward
when the risers jerked me into an upright position and the chute opened. This time I saved
the rip cord. I pulled the flashlight from my
belt and was playing it down towards the top
of the fog when I heard the plane's engine pick
up. When I jumped it had practically stopped
dead and I had neglected to cut the switches.
Apparently when the ship nosed down an additional supply of gasoline drained to the carburetor. Soon she came into sight, about a quarter
mile away and headed in the general direction
of my parachute. I put the flashlight in a
pocket of my flying suit preparatory to slipping
the parachute out of the way if necessary. The
plane was making a left spiral of about a mile
diameter, and passed approximately 300 yards
away from my chute, leaving me on the outside
of the circle. I was undecided as to whether
the plane or I was descending the more rapidly
and glided my chute away from the spiral path

of the ship as rapidly as I could. The ship passed completely out of sight, but reappeared in a few seconds, its rate of descent being about the same as that of the parachute. I counted the five spirals, each one a little further away than the last, before reaching the top of the fog bank.

"When I settled into the fog I knew that the ground was within 1,000 feet and reached for the flashlight, but found it to be missing. I could see neither earth nor stars and had no idea what kind of territory was below. I crossed my legs to keep from straddling a branch or wire, guarded my face with my hands and waited. Presently I saw the outline of the ground and a moment later was down in a cornfield. The corn was over my head and the chute was lying on top of the corn stalks. I hurriedly packed it and started down a corn row. The ground visibility was about 100 yards. In a few minutes I came to a stubble field and some wagon tracks which I followed to a farmyard a quarter mile away. After reaching the farmyard I noticed auto headlights playing over the roadside. Thinking that someone might have located the wreck of the plane I walked over to the car. The occupants asked whether I had heard an airplane crash and it required some time to explain to them that I had been piloting the plane, and yet was searching for it myself. I had to display the parachute as evidence before they were thoroughly convinced. The farmer was sure, as were most others in a 3-mile radius, that the ship had just missed his house and crashed nearby. In fact, he could locate within a few rods the spot where he heard it hit the ground, and we spent an unsuccessful quarter hour hunting for the wreck in that vicinity before going to the farmhouse to arrange for a searching party and telephone St. Louis and Chicago.

"I had just put in the long distance calls when the phone rang and we were notified that the plane had been found in a cornfield over two miles away. It took several minutes to reach the site of the crash, due to the necessity of slow driving through the fog, and a small crowd had already assembled when we arrived. The plane was wound up in a ball-shaped mass. It had narrowly missed one farmhouse and had hooked its left wing in a grain shock a quarter mile beyond. The ship had landed on the left wing and wheel and skidded along the ground for 80 yards, going through one fence before coming to rest in the edge of a cornfield about 100 yards short of a barn. The mail pit was laid open and one sack of mail was on the ground. The mail, however, was uninjured.

"The sheriff from Ottawa arrived, and we took the mail to the Ottawa Post Office to be entrained at 3:30 A.M. for Chicago."

When the wreck was inspected a few days later it was discovered that a mechanic had removed the 110 gallon gasoline tank to repair a leak and had replaced it with an 85 gallon tank without notifying anyone of the change. Consequently instead of being able to return to our field at Peoria, Ill., and clear visibility, I ran out of fuel while still over the fog bank.

The circumstances surrounding my fourth emergency parachute jump were almost similar to those of the third. I took off from the Lambert-St. Louis Field at 4:20 P.M., made a five minute stop at Springfield, Ill., an hour later to take on mail, and then headed for Peoria. Weather reports telephoned to St. Louis earlier in the afternoon gave flying conditions as entirely passable. About twenty-five miles north of Springfield darkness was encountered, the ceiling had lowered to around 400 feet and a light snow was falling. At South Pekin the forward visibility of ground lights from a 150 ft. altitude was less than half a mile, and over Pekin the town lights were indistinct from 200 ft. above. After passing Pekin the plane was flown at an altimeter reading of 600 feet for about five minutes, when the lightness of the haze below indicated that it was over Peoria. Twice I could see lights on the ground and I descended to less than 200 feet before they disappeared from view. I tried to bank around one group of lights, but was unable to turn quickly enough to keep in sight.

After circling in the vicinity of Peoria for 30 minutes, I decided to try and find better weather conditions by flying northeast towards Chicago. I had ferried a ship from Chicago to St. Louis in the early afternoon, at which time the ceiling and visibility were much better near Chicago than anywhere else along the route. Enough gasoline for about an hour and ten minutes' flying remained in the gas tank, and 20 minutes in the reserve, hardly enough to return to St. Louis even had I been able to navigate directly to the field by dead reckoning and flying blind the greater portion of the way. The territory towards Chicago was much more favorable for a night landing than that around St. Louis.

For the next half hour the flight northeast was at about 2000 feet altitude and then at 600 feet.

There were now numerous breaks in the clouds and occasionally ground lights could be seen from over 500 feet. After passing over the light of a small town a fairly clear space in the clouds was encountered. I pulled up to about 600 feet, released the parachute flare, whipped the ship around to get into the wind and under the flare which lit at once. Instead of floating down slowly, however, it dropped like a rock. I could see the ground for only an instant and then there was total darkness. Meantime the ship was in a steep bank, and being blinded by the intense light I had trouble righting it. An effort to find the ground with the wing lights was in vain as their glare was worse than useless in the haze.

When about ten minutes of gas remained in the pressure tank and still not the faintest outline of any object on the ground could be seen, I decided to leave the ship rather than attempt to land blindly. I turned back southwest toward less populated country and started climbing in an attempt to get over the clouds before jumping. The main tank went dry at 7:50 P.M. and the reserve twenty minutes later. The altimeter then registered approximately 14,000 feet, yet the top of the clouds was apparently several thousand feet higher. Rolling the stabilizer back, I cut out the switches, pulled the ship up into a stall and was about to go over the right side of the cockpit when the right wing began to drop. In this position the plane would gather speed and spiral to the right, possibly striking the parachute after its first turn. I returned to the controls, righted the plane and then dove over the left side of the cockpit while the air speed registered about 70 miles per hour and the altimeter 13,000 feet. The rip cord was pulled immediately after clearing the stabilizer. The Irving chute functioned perfectly. I left the ship head first and was falling in this position when the risers whipped me around into an upright position and the chute opened. The last I saw of the DH was as it disappeared into the clouds

just after the chute opened.   It was snowing and
very cold.   For the first minute or so the parachute descended smoothly and then commenced
an excessive oscillation which continued for
about five minutes and which could not be
checked.   The first indication of the nearness of
the chute to the ground was a gradual darken-
ing of the space below.   The snow had turned
to rain and, although the chute was thoroughly
soaked, its oscillation had greatly decreased.   I
directed the beam from my 500 ft. spotlight
downward, but the ground appeared so suddenly that I landed directly on top of a barbed
wire fence without seeing it.   The fence helped
to break the fall and the barbs did not penetrate
my heavy flying suit.   The chute was blown
over the fence and was held open for some time
by the gusts of wind before collapsing.

After rolling the chute into its pack I started
towards the nearest light.   I soon came to a
road, walked about a mile to the town of Covell,
Ill., and telephoned a report to St. Louis.   The

only information I could obtain in regard to the crashed plane was from one of a group of farmers in the general store, who stated that his neighbor had heard the plane crash but could only guess at its general direction. An hour's search proved without avail. I left instructions to place a guard over the mail in case the plane was found before I returned and went to Chicago for another ship. On arriving over Covell the next morning I found the wreck with a small crowd gathered around it, less than 500 feet back of the house where I had left my parachute the night before. The nose and the wheels had struck the ground at the same time, and after sliding along for about 75 feet it had piled up in a pasture beside a hedge fence. One wheel had come off and was standing inflated against the wall on the inside of a hog house a hundred yards further on. It had gone through two fences and the wall of the house. The wings were badly splintered, but the tubular fuselage, although badly bent in places, had held its gen-

eral form even in the mail pit.   The parachute
from the flare was hanging on the tailskid.

There were three sacks of mail in the plane.
One, a full bag from St. Louis, had been split
open and some of the mail oil-soaked but legible.
The other two bags were only partially full and
were undamaged.

It was just about at this time, or shortly after,
that I first began to think about a New York-
Paris flight.   But before discussing the events
leading up to that flight, it might be well to say
a few words about the future possibilities of
commercial aviation.

In comparing aviation to other forms of
transportation it should be born in mind that the
flying machine has been in existence less than
twenty-five years.   The Wright Brothers made
their first flight at Kitty Hawk, North Carolina,
in 1903.   Yet in 1927 air liners are operating
regularly over long distances and under all
conditions.

The first airplane was a frail machine capable

of operation only in good weather. Even with the utmost care, flying in the early days of aviation was a dangerous profession at best.

Today the properly operated commercial airline compares favorably in safety with any other means of transportation.

Shipping has reached its present stage after thousands of years of development. Railroads, less than a century ago, stopped their trains at night on the grounds that operation in darkness was unsafe. Automobiles, after nearly forty years of progress, are still dependent on good roads.

The airplane, in less than quarter of a century, has taken its place among the most important methods of travel and now, where time is paramount and territory inaccessible, it stands at the head of its competition.

Development up to the present time has been largely military. The cost of aeronautical engineering and construction has been so great that commercial companies have not been able to af-

© *Wide World Photos*

THE U. S. S. "MEMPHIS," FLAGSHIP ON WHICH THE AUTHOR RETURNED TO AMERICA

WASHINGTON, D. C.—COMING DOWN THE GANGPLANK OF THE U. S. S. "MEMPHIS," FOLLOWED BY HIS MOTHER

ford to experiment with their own designs.
While the airplane was still an experiment the
financial returns from aeronautical projects were
only too often less than the cost of operation.
Consequently the early development was largely
sponsored by the government, with the result
that the planes were designed for use in warfare
rather than for safety and economy of operation.
Extreme safety, in the military machine, must be
sacrificed for maneuverability. Economy of
operation was replaced by military design.

Commercial aviation, in the United States, has
been retarded in the past by lack of government
subsidy, but the very lack of that subsidy will be
one of its greatest assets in the future. A sub-
sidized airline is organized with the subsidy as a
very large consideration. The organization ex-
ists on the subsidy and its growth is regulated
by the subsidy. Years will be required before
the point of independence is reached and the re-
ceipts become larger than the expenditures.

On the other hand, an airline organized without regard to an external income is in a position to expand along with the demands for service. If the traffic becomes great enough to require more or bigger planes, a larger profit ensues, instead of an increased subsidy being required or the fare being raised to hold down the demand.

The airplane has now advanced to the stage where the demands of commerce are sufficient to warrant the building of planes without regard to military usefulness. And with the advent of the purely commercial airplane comes an economy of operation which places operating organizations on a sound financial basis.

Undoubtedly in a few years the United States will be covered with a net work of passenger, mail and express lines.

Trans-Atlantic service is still in the future. Extensive research and careful study will be required before any regular schedule between America and Europe can be maintained. Multi-motored flying boats with stations along the route will eventually make trans-oceanic airlines practical but their development must be based on a solid foundation of experience and equipment.

IX

THE trans-Atlantic non-stop flight between New York and Paris was first brought into public consideration by Raymond Orteig who, in 1919, issued a challenge to the Aeronautical world by offering a prize of $25,000 to the first successful entrant. Details of the flight were placed in the hands of the National Aeronautic Association and a committee was appointed to form and administer the rules of the undertaking.

I first considered the possibility of the New York-Paris flight while flying the mail one night in the fall of 1926. Several facts soon became outstanding. The foremost was that with the modern radial air-cooled motor, high lift airfoils, and lightened construction, it would not only be possible to reach Paris but, under normal conditions, to land with a large reserve of fuel and have a high factor of safety throughout the entire trip as well.

I found that there were a number of public spirited men in St. Louis sufficiently interested in aviation to finance such a project, and in December 1926 I made a trip to New York to obtain information concerning planes, motors, and other details connected with the undertaking.

In connection with any important flight there are a number of questions which must be decided at the start, among the most important of which are the type of plane and the number of motors to be used. A monoplane, although just coming into general use in the United States, is much more efficient than a biplane for certain purposes due to the lack of interference between wings, and consequently can carry a greater load per square foot of surface at a higher speed. A single motored plane, while it is more liable to forced landings than one with three motors, has much less head resistance and consequently a greater cruising range. Also there is three times the chance of motor failure with a tri-motored ship, for the failure of one motor during the first part of the flight, although it would not cause a forced landing, would at least necessitate dropping part of the fuel and returning for another start.

The reliability of the modern air-cooled radial engine is so great that the chances of an immediate forced landing due to motor failure with a single motor, would in my opinion, be more than counterbalanced by the longer cruising range and consequent ability to reach the objective in the face of unfavorable conditions.

After careful investigation I decided that a single motored monoplane was, for my purpose, the type most suited to a long distance flight, and after two more trips to the east coast and several conferences in St. Louis, an order was placed with the Ryan Airlines of San Diego, California, on February 28, 1927, for a plane equipped with a Wright Whirlwind J. 5. C. 200-H.P. radial air-cooled motor and Pioneer navigating instruments including the Earth Inductor Compass.

I went to San Diego to place the order and remained in California during the entire construction of the plane.

The personnel of the Ryan Airlines at once caught the spirit of the undertaking, and during the two months of construction the organization labored as it never had before. Day and night, seven days a week, the structure grew from a few lengths of steel tubing to one of the most efficient planes that has ever taken the air. During this time it was not unusual for the men to work twenty-four hours without rest, and on one occasion Donald Hall, the Chief Engineer, was over his drafting table for thirty-six hours.

I spent the greater part of the construction period working out the details of navigation and plotting the course, with its headings and variations, on the maps and charts. After working out the track on the gnomonic and Mercators charts, I checked over the entire distance from New York to Paris with the nautical tables. The flight from San Diego to St. Louis and from St. Louis to New York was comparatively simple, and I took the courses directly from the state maps.

From New York to Paris I worked out a great circle, changing course every hundred miles or approximately every hour. I had decided to replace the weight of a navigator with extra fuel, and this gave me about three hundred miles additional range. Although the total distance was 3610 miles, the water gap between Newfoundland and Ireland was only about 1850 miles, and under normal conditions I could have arrived on the coast of Europe over three hundred miles off of my course and still have had enough fuel remaining to reach Paris; or I might have struck the coastline as far north as Northern Scandinavia, or as far south as Southern Spain and landed without danger to myself or the plane, even though I had not reached my destination. With these facts in view, I believed the additional reserve of fuel to be more important on this flight than the accuracy of celestial navigation.

For the flight from San Diego to St. Louis and New York I carried maps of the individual states and one of the United States with the course plotted on each. For the flight from New York to Paris I had two hydrographic charts of the North Atlantic Ocean containing the great circle course and its bearing at intervals of one hundred miles. In addition to these charts, I had a map of each state, territory and country passed over. This included maps of Connecticut, Rhode Island, Massachusetts, Nova Scotia, Newfoundland, Ireland, England and France. Also a map of Europe.

I expected to be able to locate my position approximately on the coast of Europe by the terraine. Ireland is somewhat mountainous; England rather hilly on the southern end; France is a lowland along the coast; Spain is mountainous.

Therefore the coastline should indicate the country, and my accurate position could be obtained by the contours of that coastline and by the position of towns, rivers and railroads.

During the time of construction it was necessary to arrange for all equipment to be carried on the flight; including equipment for emergency use in a forced landing. After the first few hours there would be enough air in the fuel tanks to keep the ship afloat for some time. I also carried an air raft which could be inflated in several minutes and which could weather a fairly rough sea.

In addition to food for the actual flight, I carried five tins of concentrated Army rations each of which contained one day's food and which could be made to last much longer if necessary. I carried two canteens of water; one containing a quart for use during the actual flight and the other containing a gallon for emergency. In addition to this water, I had an Armburst cup which is a device for condensing the moisture from human breath into drinking water. The cup is cloth covered and contains a series of baffle plates through which the breath is blown. The cup is immersed in water and then removed and blown through. The evaporation of the water on the outside cools the cup walls and baffle plates on which the breath moisture collects and runs down to the bottom of the cup.

The following is a list of the equipment carried on the flight:

- 2 Flashlights
- 1 Ball of string
- 1 Ball of cord
- 1 Hunting Knife
- 4 Red flares sealed in rubber tubes
- 1 Match safe with matches
- 1 larger needle
- 1 Canteen—4 qts.
- 1   "   —1 qt.
- 1 Armburst Cup
- 1 Air Raft with pump and repair kit
- 5 Cans of Army emergency rations
- 2 Air cushions
- 1 Hack saw blade

Near the end of April the factory work was completed and early one morning, the 46 ft. wing was taken out of the second floor of the factory onto the top of a freight car and then lowered to a waiting truck by means of a gasoline crane. A few days later the plane was completely assembled in its hangar, and on April 28th, or sixty days after the order had been placed, I gave "The Spirit of St. Louis" her test flight. The actual performance was above the theoretical. The plane was off the ground in six and one-eighth seconds, or in 165 feet, and was carrying over 400 lbs. in extra gas tanks and equipment. The high speed was 130 M.P.H. and the climb excellent.

The load tests were made from the old Camp Kearney parade grounds near San Diego. At daybreak, one foggy morning, I took off from the field at Dutch Flats and headed for the Army's three kilometer speed course along Coronado Strand. The visibility became extremely bad over San Diego harbor and I was forced to

land at Rockwell Field, North Island, and wait
for the fog to lift before running the speed tests.
The sun soon dispelled the fog and I took the
plane four times over the speed course at an average of 128 M.P.H. in a slight cross wind.   I
was carrying about 25 gals. of gasoline and over
400 lbs. of extra tanks and equipment.   On the
way to Camp Kearney I ran a number of tests
on the relation of motor R.P.M. to air speed, and
by the time I reached the old parade-grounds'
field I had collected quite a bit of valuable test
data.

I decided to run one more test before landing
and had it about half way completed when I
allowed the data board to come too close to the
window where a gust of air carried it out of the
cockpit.   I was flying over mesquite, over five
miles from Camp Kearney, at about a 1200-foot
altitude at the time, and could only spiral around
and watch the board flutter down into the top
of a mesquite bush.   There was a small clearing
about 200 yards from the bush, in which it was

possible to land a slow ship. I landed at Camp Kearney and sent for one of the cabin Hisso Standards used by the Ryan Airlines for their passenger service between San Diego and Los Angeles. When the Standard arrived I flew over and landed in the clearing near the lost board which was clearly visible from the air; but, after a fifteen minute search, I was unable to locate it from the ground in the thick mesquite. So I took off my coat and spread it over the top of another bush, then took the air again with the Standard to locate the board in relation to the coat.

I had no difficulty in locating them both and found them to be about fifty yards apart. I landed again but could not locate the board, so moved my coat to the spot where I thought it should be and took off again. This time I had placed the coat within twenty feet of the data board, but it required several minutes' search in the thick mesquite to finally locate it.

After I returned to Camp Kearney with the

Standard, we made preparations for the weight tests of the Spirit of St. Louis.

The tests were to be made starting with a light load and increasing the weight carried by about fifty gallons of fuel for each test up to three hundred gallons, which was to be the maximum load tested. The plane passed its tests easily and took off with three hundred gallons in twenty seconds or 1026 feet, and made a maximum speed of 124 miles per hour. The tests were made in a quartering wind varying from two to nine miles per hour and at an elevation of about six hundred feet above sea level.

The final flight ended at dusk and the plane was left under guard on the field over night. The next morning, after most of the gasoline had been drained, I flew it back to Dutch Flats where final preparations were made for the flight to St. Louis.

I was delayed four days at San Diego by a general storm area over the United States that would greatly jeopardize the success of an overnight non-stop flight to St. Louis. From this flight I expected to obtain some very important data for use on the final hop from New York.

On the afternoon of May 9th, Dean Blake, Chief of the San Diego Weather Bureau, predicted favorable flying conditions for the succeeding day. The next morning I took the plane to Rockwell Field and at 3:55 P.M. Pacific time, I took off from North Island with 250 gallons of gasoline for the flight to St. Louis, escorted by two Army observation planes and one of the Ryan monoplanes. We circled North Island and San Diego, then headed on a compass course for St. Louis.

The ship passed over the first ridge of mountains, about 4,000 feet, very easily with reduced throttle. The escorting planes turned back at the mountains and I passed on over the desert and the Salton Sea alone. And at sunset I was over the deserts and mountains of Western Arizona.

The moon was well above the horizon and with

WASHINGTON, D. C.—CHARLES EVANS HUGHES CONFERS THE CROSS OF HONOR FROM THE
UNITED STATES FLAG ASSOCIATION

© *Wide World Photos*

WASHINGTON, D. C. —AT THE TOMB OF "THE UNKNOWN SOLDIER," AT ARLINGTON CEMETERY

the exception of a short period before dawn I was able to distinguish the contour of the country the entire night. I flew a compass course, passing alternately over snow-capped ridges, deserts, and fertile valleys. One of the mountain ranges was over 12,000 feet high and completely snow covered. I cleared this range by about 500 feet and went on over the plains beyond.

The mountains passed quickly and long before daybreak I was flying over the prairies of Western Kansas. At dawn I located my position about twenty miles south of the course, just east of Wichita, Kansas. At 8:00 A.M. Central Standard time, I passed over Lambert Field and landed at 8:20 A.M., May 11th, fourteen hours and twenty-five minutes after leaving the Pacific Coast.

The weather during the entire distance had been exactly as Dean Blake had predicted.

At 8:13 the next morning (May 12th) I took off from Lambert Field for New York. The wind was west and the weather clear for the greater part of the distance. Over the Alleghanys, however, the sky was overcast and some of the mountain tops were in low hanging clouds and I followed the passes.

At 5:33 P.M. New York Daylight Saving time, I landed at Curtiss Field, Long Island.

X

NEW YORK TO PARIS

A T New York we checked over the plane,
engine and instruments, which required
several short flights over the field.

When the plane was completely inspected and
ready for the trans-Atlantic flight, there were
dense fogs reported along the coast and over
Nova Scotia and Newfoundland, in addition to
a storm area over the North Atlantic.

On the morning of May 19th, a light rain was
falling and the sky was overcast. Weather reports from land stations and ships along the
great circle course were unfavorable and there
was apparently no prospect of taking off for
Paris for several days at least. In the morning
I visited the Wright plant at Paterson, New
Jersey, and had planned to attend a theatre per-

213

formance in New York that evening. But at about six o'clock I received a special report from the New York Weather Bureau. A high pressure area was over the entire North Atlantic and the low pressure over Nova Scotia and Newfoundland was receding. It was apparent that the prospects of the fog clearing up were as good as I might expect for some time to come. The North Atlantic should be clear with only local storms on the coast of Europe. The moon had just passed full and the percentage of days with fog over Newfoundland and the Grand Banks was increasing so that there seemed to be no advantage in waiting longer.

We went to Curtiss Field as quickly as possible and made arrangements for the barograph to be sealed and installed, and for the plane to be serviced and checked.

We decided partially to fill the fuel tanks in the hangar before towing the ship on a truck to Roosevelt Field, which adjoins Curtiss on the east, where the servicing would be completed.

I left the responsibility for conditioning the plane in the hands of the men on the field while I went into the hotel for about two and one-half hours of rest; but at the hotel there were several more details which had to be completed and I was unable to get any sleep that night.

I returned to the field before daybreak on the morning of the twentieth. A light rain was falling which continued until almost dawn; consequently we did not move the ship to Roosevelt Field until much later than we had planned, and the take-off was delayed from daybreak until nearly eight o'clock.

At dawn the shower had passed, although the sky was overcast, and occasionally there would be some slight precipitation. The tail of the plane was lashed to a truck and escorted by a number of motorcycle police. The slow trip from Curtiss to Roosevelt was begun.

The ship was placed at the extreme west end of the field heading along the east and west runway, and the final fueling commenced.

About 7:40 A.M. the motor was started and at 7:52 I took off on the flight for Paris.

The field was a little soft due to the rain during the night and the heavily loaded plane gathered speed very slowly. After passing the half-way mark, however, it was apparent that I would be able to clear the obstructions at the end. I passed over a tractor by about fifteen feet and a telephone line by about twenty, with a fair reserve of flying speed. I believe that the ship would have taken off from a hard field with at least five hundred pounds more weight.

I turned slightly to the right to avoid some high trees on a hill directly ahead, but by the time I had gone a few hundred yards I had sufficient altitude to clear all obstructions and throttled the engine down to 1750 R.P.M. I took up a compass course at once and soon reached Long Island Sound where the Curtiss Oriole with its photographer, which had been escorting me, turned back.

The haze soon cleared and from Cape Cod

through the southern half of Nova Scotia the weather and visibility were excellent. I was flying very low, sometimes as close as ten feet from the trees and water.

On the three hundred mile stretch of water between Cape Cod and Nova Scotia I passed within view of numerous fishing vessels.

The northern part of Nova Scotia contained a number of storm areas and several times I flew through cloudbursts.

As I neared the northern coast, snow appeared in patches on the ground and far to the eastward the coastline was covered with fog.

For many miles between Nova Scotia and Newfoundland the ocean was covered with caked ice but as I approached the coast the ice disappeared entirely and I saw several ships in this area.

I had taken up a course for St. Johns, which is south of the great Circle from New York to Paris, so that there would be no question of the fact that I had passed Newfoundland in case I was forced down in the north Atlantic.

I passed over numerous icebergs after leaving
St. Johns, but saw no ships except near the coast.

Darkness set in about 8:15 and a thin, low fog
formed over the sea through which the white
bergs showed up with surprising clearness. This
fog became thicker and increased in height until
within two hours I was just skimming the top of
storm clouds at about ten thousand feet. Even at
this altitude there was a thick haze through which
only the stars directly overhead could be seen.

There was no moon and it was very dark. The
tops of some of the storm clouds were several
thousand feet above me and at one time, when I
attempted to fly through one of the larger clouds,
sleet started to collect on the plane and I was
forced to turn around and get back into clear air
immediately and then fly around any clouds
which I could not get over.

The moon appeared on the horizon after about
two hours of darkness; then the flying was much
less complicated.

Dawn came at about 1 A.M. New York time

and the temperature had risen until there was practically no remaining danger of sleet.

Shortly after sunrise the clouds became more broken although some of them were far above me and it was often necessary to fly through them, navigating by instruments only.

As the sun became higher, holes appeared in the fog. Through one the open water was visible, and I dropped down until less than a hundred feet above the waves. There was a strong wind blowing from the northwest and the ocean was covered with white caps.

After a few miles of fairly clear weather the ceiling lowered to zero and for nearly two hours I flew entirely blind through the fog at an altitude of about 1500 feet. Then the fog raised and the water was visible again.

On several more occasions it was necessary to fly by instrument for short periods; then the fog broke up into patches. These patches took on forms of every description. Numerous shore-lines appeared, with trees perfectly outlined against the horizon. In fact, the mirages were so natural that, had I not been in mid-Atlantic and known that no land existed along my route, I would have taken them to be actual islands.

As the fog cleared I dropped down closer to the water, sometimes flying within ten feet of the waves and seldom higher than two hundred.

There is a cushion of air close to the ground or water through which a plane flies with less effort than when at a higher altitude, and for hours at a time I took advantage of this factor.

Also, it was less difficult to determine the wind drift near the water. During the entire flight the wind was strong enough to produce white caps on the waves. When one of these formed, the foam would be blown off, showing the wind's direction and approximate velocity. This foam remained on the water long enough for me to obtain a general idea of my drift.

During the day I saw a number of porpoises and a few birds but no ships, although I under-

stand that two different boats reported me passing over.

The first indication of my approach to the
European Coast was a small fishing boat which
I first noticed a few miles ahead and slightly to
the south of my course. There were several of
these fishing boats grouped within a few miles of
each other.

I flew over the first boat without seeing any
signs of life. As I circled over the second, however, a man's face appeared, looking out of the
cabin window.

I have carried on short conversations with people on the ground by flying low with throttled
engine, shouting a question, and receiving the
answer by some signal. When I saw this fisher-
man I decided to try to get him to point towards
land. I had no sooner made the decision than the
futility of the effort became apparent. In all
likelihood he could not speak English, and even
if he could he would undoubtedly be far too
astounded to answer. However, I circled again

and closing the throttle as the plane passed within a few feet of the boat I shouted, "Which way is Ireland?" Of course the attempt was useless, and I continued on my course.

Less than an hour later a rugged and semi-mountainous coastline appeared to the northeast. I was flying less than two hundred feet from the water when I sighted it. The shore was fairly distinct and not over ten or fifteen miles away. A light haze coupled with numerous local storm areas had prevented my seeing it from a long distance.

The coastline came down from the north, curved over towards the east. I had very little doubt that it was the southwestern end of Ireland but in order to make sure I changed my course towards the nearest point of land.

I located Cape Valentia and Dingle Bay, then resumed my compass course towards Paris.

After leaving Ireland I passed a number of steamers and was seldom out of sight of a ship.

In a little over two hours the coast of England appeared. My course passed over Southern England and a little south of Plymouth; then across the English Channel, striking France over Cherbourg.

The English farms were very impressive from the air in contrast to ours in America. They appeared extremely small and unusually neat and tidy with their stone and hedge fences.

I was flying at about a fifteen hundred foot altitude over England and as I crossed the Channel and passed over Cherbourg, France, I had probably seen more of that part of Europe than many native Europeans. The visibility was good and the country could be seen for miles around.

People who have taken their first flight often remark that no one knows what the locality he lives in is like until he has seen it from above. Countries take on different characteristics from the air.

The sun went down shortly after passing

Cherbourg and soon the beacons along the Paris-London airway became visible.

I first saw the lights of Paris a little before ten P.M., or five P.M. New York time, and a few minutes later I was circling the Eiffel Tower at an altitude of about four thousand feet.

The lights of Le Bourget were plainly visible, but appeared to be very close to Paris. I had understood that the field was farther from the city, so continued out to the northeast into the country for four or five miles to make sure that there was not another field farther out which might be Le Bourget. Then I returned and spiralled down closer to the lights. Presently I could make out long lines of hangars, and the roads appeared to be jammed with cars.

I flew low over the field once, then circled around into the wind and landed.

After the plane stopped rolling I turned it around and started to taxi back to the lights. The entire field ahead, however, was covered with thousands of people all running towards my ship.

When the first few arrived, I attempted to get them to hold the rest of the crowd back, away from the plane, but apparently no one could understand, or would have been able to conform to my request if he had.

I cut the switch to keep the propeller from killing some one, and attempted to organize an impromptu guard for the plane. The impossibility of any immediate organization became apparent, and when parts of the ship began to crack from the pressure of the multitude I decided to climb out of the cockpit in order to draw the crowd away.

Speaking was impossible; no words could be heard in the uproar and nobody apparently cared to hear any. I started to climb out of the cockpit, but as soon as one foot appeared through the door I was dragged the rest of the way without assistance on my part.

For nearly half an hour I was unable to touch the ground, during which time I was ardently carried around in what seemed to be a very small area, and in every position it is possible to be in. Every one had the best of intentions but no one seemed to know just what they were.

The French military flyers very resourcefully took the situation in hand. A number of them mingled with the crowd; then, at a given signal, they placed my helmet on an American correspondent and cried: "Here is Lindbergh." That helmet on an American was sufficient evidence. The correspondent immediately became the center of attraction, and while he was being taken protestingly to the Reception Committee via a rather devious route, I managed to get inside one of the hangars.

Meanwhile a second group of soldiers and police had surrounded the plane and soon placed it out of danger in another hangar.

The French ability to handle an unusual situation with speed and capability was remarkably demonstrated that night at Le Bourget.

Ambassador Herrick extended me an invitation to remain at his Embassy while I was in

WASHINGTON, D. C.—SPEECHES AT WASHINGTON MONUMENT. THE PRESIDENT AT
COLONEL LINDBERGH'S RIGHT

FROM THE TOP OF WASHINGTON MONUMENT

Paris, which I gladly accepted. But grateful as I was at the time, it did not take me long to realize that a kind Providence had placed me in Ambassador Herrick's hands. The ensuing days found me in situations that I had certainly never expected to be in and in which I relied on Ambassador Herrick's sympathetic aid.

These situations were brought about by the whole-hearted welcome to me—an American —that touched me beyond any point that any words can express. I left France with a debt of gratitude which, though I cannot repay it, I shall always remember. If the French people had been acclaiming their own gallant airmen, Nungesser and Coli, who were lost only after fearlessly departing in the face of conditions insurmountably greater than those that confronted me, their enthusiastic welcome and graciousness could not have been greater.

In Belgium as well, I was received with a warmth which reflected more than simply a passing curiosity in a trans-Atlantic flight, but which was rather a demonstration by the people of their interest in a new means of transportation which eventually would bring still closer together the new world and the old. Their welcome, too, will be a cherished memory for all time.

In England, I experienced one final unforgettable demonstration of friendship for an American. That spontaneous wonderful reception during my brief visit seemed typical of what I had always heard of the good sportsmanship of the English.

My words to all those friends in Europe are inadequate, but my feelings of appreciation are boundless.

Conclusion

When I was contemplating the flight to Paris I looked forward to making a short tour of Europe with especial regard to the various airports and aeronautical activities.

After I arrived, however, the necessity for returning to America in the near future became apparent and, after a consultation with Ambassador Houghton, who informed me that President Coolidge was sending the cruiser *Memphis* to Cherbourg for my return journey to America, I flew the "Spirit of St. Louis" to Gosport early one morning. There it was dismantled and crated, through the courtesy of the Royal Air Force which also placed a Woodcock pursuit plane at my disposal.

I returned to London in the Woodcock and a few days later flew to Paris in another R.A.F. machine of the same type.

I remained overnight in Paris, and early the next morning flew a French Breguet to Cherbourg where the cruiser *Memphis* was waiting.

Admiral Burrage met me at the dock, and after going aboard the *Memphis* I became acquainted with Captain Lackey and the officers of the ship. During the trip across they extended every courtesy and did everything within their power to make the voyage a pleasant one.

A description of my welcome back to the United States would, in itself, be sufficient to fill a larger volume than this. I am not an author by profession, and my pen could never express the gratitude which I feel towards the American people.

The voyage up the Potomac and to the Monument Grounds in Washington; up the Hudson River and along Broadway; over the Mississippi and to St. Louis—to do justice to these occasions would require a far greater writer than myself.

Washington, New York, and finally St. Louis and home. Each of these cities has left me with an impression that I shall never forget, and a debt of gratitude which I can never repay.

PUBLISHER'S NOTE

When Lindbergh came to tell the story of his welcome at Paris, London, Brussels, Washington, New York and St. Louis he found himself up against a tougher problem than flying the Atlantic.

He wanted to speak from his heart his appreciation for all the kindness and enthusiasm that had been shown him. But when he began to write he found that fitting words would not come. Somehow it wasn't a story for him to tell.

So the publishers agreed to his suggestion that this part of the record be put in the third person by a writer he might choose. As a result much in the way of illuminating speeches and other important matter is included that Lindbergh would have been loath to use.

AUTHOR'S NOTE

I have asked Fitzhugh Green to write a brief account of my various receptions not only because I think he has caught the spirit of what I have tried to do for aviation, but because I trust his judgment in selection of material.

Charles A. Lindbergh

A LITTLE OF WHAT THE WORLD THOUGHT OF LINDBERGH

BY

FITZHUGH GREEN

I

PARIS

CHARLES A. LINDBERGH was the "dark horse" of the New York to Paris flight; also he flew alone. These two facts, combined with the tragic disappearance of the French trans-Atlantic fliers, Nungesser and Coli, shortly before he left New York, emphasized the suspense with which Paris awaited his arrival.

He landed safely on a dark night about on schedule time. This was the culmination of what might be called the mechanical aspect of his success.

In consequence of these unique but rather simple circumstances it was natural that there should follow a good deal of notoriety for the flier. Already the so-called "trans-Atlantic Air Race" had received much advertising. Several planes had been grooming for the long flight; and there had been much speculation about the practicability of such an effort. Lindbergh's landing figuratively rang the bell as the winner came under the wire.

The first man over was bound to be recognized as an audacious pioneer. Without regard for his character, creed or aspirations the world was going to come forward and say "Well done!"

The first man to fly from New York to Paris was bound to be fêted and decorated. He would tell the story of his flight and there would be ephemeral discussion of its bearing on the future of aviation. Wild speculation about the world being on the brink of a great air age would follow.

The first man to fly from New York to Paris was bound to excite the admiration of his own

© *Wide World Photos*

WASHINGTON, D. C.—AT ARLINGTON CEMETERY

COPY OF THE $25,000 CHECK PRESENTED BY RAYMOND ORTEIG

NEW YORK CITY—RECEIVING THE ORTEIG PRIZE MEDAL.   MR. ORTEIG IS
STANDING IN THE CENTRE BETWEEN COLONEL SCOTT AND MYSELF

countrymen. He would be met on his return by committees, have to make some speeches at banquets and receive appropriate decorations for his valor.

The first man to fly from New York to Paris would write several magazine articles and a book. He might make some money by lecturing. He would be offered contracts for moving pictures, jobs as manager of something or other, and honorary memberships in a hundred organizations of more or less doubtful value.

Then someone would break a homerun record or commit a murder; whereupon the world would forget with pitiless promptness the first man to fly the broad Atlantic.

Who, by the way, can name the dauntless pilots that circled the globe by air not so many months ago?

The reason Lindbergh's story is different is that when his plane came to a halt on Le Bourget field that black night in Paris, Lindbergh the man kept on going.

The phenomenon of Lindbergh took its start with his flight across the ocean; but in its entirety it was almost as distinct from that flight as though he had never flown at all.

It is probable that in the three ensuing weeks Lindbergh loosed the greatest torrent of mass emotion ever witnessed in human history.

This narrative is a record of events, not an analysis. It therefore cannot pretend to explain the "phenomenon of Lindbergh." Whether it was his modesty or his looks or his refusal to be tempted by money or by fame that won him such a following we cannot say. Perhaps the world was ripe for a youth with a winning smile to flash across its horizon and by the brilliance of his achievement momentarily dim the ugliness of routine business, politics and crime. Many said that his sudden meteor-like appearance from obscurity was an act of Providence.

Whatever the reason for it all, the fact remains that there was a definite "phenomenon of Lindbergh" quite the like of which the world had

never seen. This strange phenomenon is the
opening fact of our simple narrative of events
culled from a list far too long to include in the
space allowed.

All who followed press accounts of the flier's
adventures after landing agree that his "meteor"
did not glow in its full radiance at first. There
was a faint but unmistakable artificiality in the
news reports on this side of the Atlantic immediately following his arrival in Paris. To be sure,
unstinted praise was poured on his courage and
on the skill of his unprecedented flight. But the
true Lindbergh had not yet impressed itself
upon America.

His personality caught the French at the very
moment when their natural enthusiasm for his
deed was at its height. It was like pushing a
swing just when it has started downward.

Two French aviation officers extricated him
from the milling crowd at Le Bourget on arrival
night and succeeded in getting him to the American Embassy where newspaper men located him

at 1:30 A.M. The journalists naturally found
the flier tired after having had practically no
sleep for nearly sixty hours. But he was far
from exhausted and he had no maudlin recital
for the pencil-pushers who so eagerly surrounded him.

He awakened near noon next day. After
breakfast he went out on a balcony in response
to crowds in the street and for the first time
after his triumph stood face to face in daylight
with citizens of France. There was a burst of
applause. As we have said, the first man to
have flown from New York to Paris, was bound
to get just this applause. Then something else
happened.

We talked to one of the Diplomatic Corps who
witnessed this first public appearance. He said:
"The people kept on cheering and clapping and
waving their hats or handkerchiefs; but I suddenly had a feeling they were applauding me-
chanically, as if their attention were rooted on
something that fascinated them.

"I glanced up at Lindbergh to see if he were doing anything he shouldn't do. No, he was just smiling and his ruddy face was alight with appreciation.

"I looked from Lindbergh to the crowd. Then I realized that something was going on right before my eyes that I couldn't see. Lindbergh's personality was reaching out and winning the French just as surely as his flight had reached out and found their city."

That was the beginning of the "phenomenon of Lindbergh." It grew in a steady crescendo as the days passed. We saw it full force in Washington. We saw it reach incredible heights in New York.

Procession of events fitted into and abetted development of the situation. There was the telephone conversation from Paris to his mother in Detroit four thousand miles away. *His mother:* the world rolled the two words around its collective tongue as might a wine connoisseur his nectar.

He called on Madame Nungesser, another mother, whose equally brave son had disappeared but a few days before in the stormy wastes of the same ocean he had crossed. Their exchange was brief, but the whole world listened and wiped away a tear. In simple compassion Lindbergh told the mother not to give up hope. You have to know the boy to feel a fraction of the reassurance he must have conveyed.

He visited the blind and crippled veterans of the great war. He smiled at them; which was enough for those who could see, who in turn ransacked their expressive tongue to explain *"le joli Lindbergh"* to those who couldn't.

He called on the President of the Republic. He was dressed in plain clothes but the meeting was full of affability on both sides, with Sheldon Whitehouse of the Embassy acting as interpreter. The President pinned the Cross of the Legion of Honor upon the lapel of the boy's borrowed suit and kissed him on both cheeks.

By this time France was alive to Lindbergh; America was waking up.

At the Aero Club of France he made his first
speech. His precise laconic diction was one more
step forward in the phenomenon of Lindbergh.
The speech was printed widely in America. The
Club was jammed that day and Minister of War
Paul Painlevé, surrounded by fifty of the leading aviators of France, received the guest of
honor. When the time came Herrick quietly
leaned over and told Lindbergh he must respond.
Whereupon the latter rose and said that Nungesser and Coli had attempted a far greater thing
than he when they took off from Paris for New
York. Their difficulties had far exceeded his.
In any event he urged France not to give up
hope. Nothing could have been more tactful.

Ambassador Herrick's speech which followed
emphasized the strengthened good-will between
France and America. "This young man from
out of the west brings you better than anything
else the spirit of America," he said. "His exploit shows you that the heart of the United
States beats for France. It was needed at this

moment that the love of these two great people should manifest itself, and it is this young boy who has brought that about. After his European trip is over he will go back to America and he will be able to tell them as no other man could that France really loves the people of the United States."

Thus was the idea of "ambassadorship without portfolio" initiated. When press and people, and especially statesmen, began to see how the current strain between France and America was slackening as a result of Lindbergh's visit, the idea grew doubly strong.

On the following day he went to a large luncheon of 600 Americans at the American Club. On Wednesday he visited the French Chamber of Deputies. There was no session in progress, yet most of the members present followed him to the reception room of the President's residence. Like ferment in wine, Lindbergh's personality was working hour by hour.

Here again the increased cordiality between

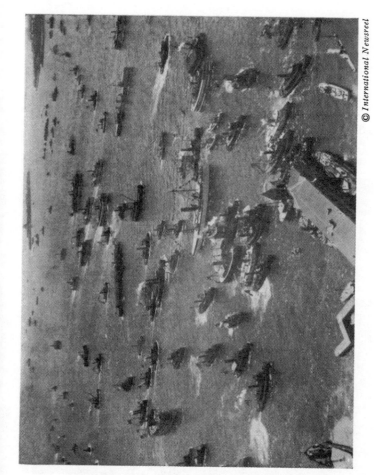

WELCOME IN NEW YORK HARBOR

© *International Newsreel*

NEW YORK CITY—RIDING UP BROADWAY

France and America became the keynote of the interchange. The adored General Gouraud said: "It is not only two continents that you have united, but the hearts of all men everywhere in admiration of the simple courage of a man who does great things. . . . You and your youth belong to that glorious band of which M. Bleriot standing here beside you was one, and which has opened the great spaces. We greet you also in the name of those others of your countrymen who, in the Lafayette Escadrille, died here for France—who, like you, helped to frame that unalterable fraternity, that indissoluble friendship which unites our two peoples."

In like vein but with an eye to practicality Lindbergh replied:

"Gentlemen, 132 years ago Benjamin Franklin was asked: 'What good is your balloon? What will it accomplish?' He replied: 'What good is a new born child?' Less than twenty years ago when I was not far advanced from infancy M. Bleriot flew across the English Channel and was asked 'What good is your aeroplane? What will it accomplish?' Today those same skeptics might ask me what good has been my flight from New York to Paris. My answer is that I believe it is the forerunner of a great air service from America to France, America to Europe, to bring our peoples nearer together in understanding and in friendship than they have ever been."

The speaker's abrupt but unmistakable sincerity made a profound impression upon his hearers.

It is impossible to do justice to the full Paris visit. Yet it is not difficult even now to sense the ever increasing aura of popularity and affection that surrounded Lindbergh wherever he went.

He lunched with Bleriot, the first man to fly across the English Channel, who presented him with a piece of the propeller of that famous plane of early days. He had a notable visit with Marshal Foch. He went to the Invalides surrounded by an admiring crowd. He went to the home of Marshal Joffre. He attended a formal lunch with Minister Briand.

Meanwhile a growing avalanche of mail was descending upon the Embassy. There were startling business offers running into millions of dollars. Cables from all parts of the world urged Lindbergh to write this or that, or agree to appear at highly remunerative rates under any and all circumstances. He did not handle this mail or accept any of these offers. He could not do the former, and he would not do the latter. But he was not cynical; only gravely dubious about the results of his original enterprise getting so far out of his control.

On Thursday of that Paris week came the official reception by the City. By this time the popularity of the boy held full sway. It is said that half a million people lined the streets through which the flier drove in company with his host, the Ambassador.

At the City Hall, Lindbergh received the Gold

Medal of the Muncipality of Paris. In a brief speech he told the Council that he believed his flight was the forerunner of a regular commercial air-service between the United States and France. He added that Nungesser and Coli would have voiced the same thought if they had landed in America.

Ambassador Herrick then made one of his finest and most widely quoted speeches. "I am not a religious man," he said, "but I believe there are certain things that happen in life which can only be described as the interpretation of a Divine Act. I would not be surprised if this flight marks the beginning of a return of that sympathy and affection which lasted 150 years between France and America. Lindbergh brought you the spirit of America in a manner in which it could never be brought in a diplomatic sack."

Next morning Lindbergh got up at daybreak and went to Le Bourget where he found a small black Nieuport 300 H.P. fighting plane awaiting him. To the delight of the French fliers as well as the populace he went aloft and began stunting with a skill and ease that stamped him once and for all an expert. Again he rose a peg in French esteem. Nor was this a studied performance any more than his modesty in bearing or his brevity in oratory were studied. It was only another integral part of the "phenomenon of Lindbergh."

At noon there was a luncheon at the Ministry of War. Later he was received by the Senators at the Luxembourg Palace. A reception and official visits followed. In the evening he attended a gala performance at the Champs Élysées Theatre.

The very recital of his festivities and honors grows monotonous.

Next day he left. About eight in the morning he motored to Le Bourget and put in three hours grooming his plane for its next flight. At noon he hopped off for Brussels, circling the Eiffel Tower and dropping a note of goodby and thanks to Paris in the Place de la Concorde on his way.

II

THE Belgian reception was one of quiet dignity. King Albert had given orders that at all costs Lindbergh must come off the field untouched.

The flier landed at the Evere Flying Field near Brussels at exactly 3.15 P.M. The crowd that greeted him was never out of hand. Prime Minister Jasper came forward at once and said: "I am happy and proud, my Captain, to be the first man in the name of Belgium to extend to you our warmest felicitations for your great exploit, which not only draws nearer our two continents, but the hearts of our people as well."

As Mr. Gibson, the new American Ambassador to Belgium, was in America at the time, his place was temporarily occupied by Mr. Dunn, Chargé d' Affaires. By him Lindbergh was presented to the Duke of Brabant, heir to the throne, who formally welcomed the visitor in the name of King Albert. Meanwhile the plane had been carefully wheeled upon a platform so that everyone might take a look at it.

After motoring to the American Embassy to change his clothes, Lindbergh laid a wreath on the tomb of Belgium's unknown soldier.

It was at the reception at the Palace that Lindbergh met his first king. King Albert treated him with a kind informality characteristic of that much-loved monarch.

Next morning, Lindbergh slept until nearly nine. Then he went out to the Evere Airdrome, where he showed his plane to King Albert and Queen Elizabeth. King Albert in his turn took the visitor to see some late types of Belgian planes and personally explained their technical features.

At noon came the civic reception at the Hotel

de Ville. When Lindbergh arrived the square was lined with troops. Burgomaster Max, with the aldermen of Brussels, was there to meet him. There was also a welcoming delegation known as the Old Volunteers of the Great War, whose members, despite their fifty years or more, had rushed in 1914 to join the colors.

Burgomaster Max made a speech in English, saying that the flight was a wonderful sporting performance. He added that because the non-stop flight from New York to Paris had appeared to be an undertaking beyond human forces, the victory was really a victory of humanity. He concluded by declaring with great feeling:

"In your glory there is glory for all men. An apparently impossible task loomed before you. You surmounted it. It is helpful and encouraging for those who think we must never despair of human effort. You must have heard many times during these five days that in crossing the ocean with your 'Spirit of St. Louis' you have done more than all the diplomats to bring closer together the different peoples. I repeat it myself. When a statement is being commonly used, a Burgomaster should not hesitate to express it again, as his function when he speaks is to reflect public opinion.

"In uniting by airway your young country with the old soil of Europe you have drawn nearer together these two continents and you have the right to claim the title of Citizen of the World. The way now open, others will follow you, as others tried in vain to precede you.

"I am thus certain, as we welcome you here, to express your own sentiments in mentioning with emotion the names of Nungesser and Coli who a few days ago, with an assurance as great as yours, started over the Atlantic but never reached their goal.

"In you the symbol of daring and courage is impossible not to admire.

"Heroes always consider what they have done as a simple matter. This is precisely because they are heroes. I salute in you, dear Captain Lindbergh, a noble son of your great nation which at an hour when civilization was in danger came to its help and with us conquered."

Lindbergh replied to this speech by saying that there were two things he looked forward to when he took off from New York—seeing France and Belgium:

"This afternoon I must leave," he went on, "I wish I could stay here weeks instead of hours. I certainly will never forget your welcome.

"Less than twenty-five years ago, the first flight was made in an airplane. It will not be many years before we have regular trans-Atlantic service. I congratulate Belgium on her remarkable progress in aviation. You have a wonderful air force here. Aviation will be one of the great forces of the future to bring nations together."

Then the Burgomaster took Lindbergh's hand and presented him with a little leather case containing a gold medal inscribed in English:

"To Captain Charles Lindbergh, the City of Brussels, May 29th, 1927."

Lindbergh left Brussels for London in the early afternoon. On his way over Belgium he paid a tribute to the American soldiers who sleep in the cemetery at Werington near Ghent. Cutting off his motor, he flew low over the field, but little above the rows of white crosses. He dropped a wreath of flowers, circled the cemetery twice, then headed out for England.

In a sense this visit to Belgium was a surer test of the man than either of the other countries. His stay was very brief; his hosts neither spoke his tongue as did the English, nor had as natural a reservoir of emotion to draw upon as did the French. Yet Lindbergh's easy dignity, his simple bearing, and always his ready smile, were as quick to earn him the permanent friendship of King and Queen as to excite the adulation of the crowd.

It was said everywhere of him when he left: "We hope he comes back some day." No traveller receives higher praise than that.

III

THE flight from Brussels was comparatively simple and there was little or no strain on the plane. The pilot steered straight across the Channel, reaching England on the southeast corner.

The weather was nearly perfect; in fact Lindbergh was never privileged during his stay in England to see a real London fog.

It did not seem long before he found himself throttling his motor above the great field at Croydon on the outskirts of London. A tremendous crowd had gathered—a crowd almost as large as that which had watched him land that memorable night at Le Bourget. And again no sooner had his wheels touched the ground than this crowd, too, made a rush for his plane. Fortunately, officials of the Royal Air Club dashed up in a motor car and got the pilot aboard just in time to rescue him from the uncontrollable enthusiasm of the throng.

As in Paris, all the carefully laid plans of the reception committee were swept aside. Even Secretary for Air, Sir Samuel Hoare, and Ambassador Houghton were swallowed up by the multitude. Later another crowd, almost as large, was found waiting at the American Embassy for a glimpse of the American air traveller.

Then came welcomed rest. Lindbergh dined with some friends of the Ambassador and went to bed early. Next morning he went direct to Croydon and found that, despite his fears, very little harm had been done to his ship save for one little hole in the wing and a landing strut that had lost two bolts.

Monday was a comparatively quiet day. There was a luncheon at the Embassy attended by many persons prominent in the government and otherwise. One war hero was perhaps especially interesting to an air man. This was Lieut.-Col. W. A. Bishop, the Canadian ace, who had brought down 72 German planes.

In the afternoon a Memorial Day service was held at St. Margaret's Church, Westminster. This honoring in England of our Civil War dead was a strange experience for the visitor. One of the veterans present, Jabez Jrayell, aged 86, had known President McKinley as a comrade in arms. After the service and sermon a procession formed, which, headed by the Stars and Stripes, moved slowly from the church to Westminster Abbey. There, Ambassador Houghton, with Lindbergh at his side, walked to a tomb and laid a wreath on which was inscribed:

"In memory of England's unknown warrior from the American people."

In the evening British newspaper men gave Lindbergh a dinner in the Abraham Lincoln room of the Savoy. On the speaker's table be-

fore the guest of honor were five sandwiches
and a half gallon jar of water. The Chairman
gravely announced: "Captain Lindbergh will
now partake of his customary meal." After a
round of laughing applause the real dinner
began.

Next morning was the 31st of May. On this
day Lindbergh was received by the King of England. King George talked to him alone for some
time about his flight, and by his conversation
showed he understood a great deal about flying.
Setting aside all precedent, he personally presented Lindbergh with the Royal Air Force
Cross. The only other Americans who ever received this cross were the crew of the NC-4, the
United States Navy plane, which crossed the
Atlantic by way of the Azores.

After his conversation with the King, Lindbergh was presented to Queen Mary. From
Buckingham Palace he went to York House to
be received by the Prince of Wales. The Prince
wanted to know what he was going to do in the

future, to which Lindbergh promptly replied: "I am going to keep on flying."

He visited Prime Minister Baldwin at Number 10 Downing Street, the little house from which so big a slice of this world is being run. Mr. Baldwin took him out on the balcony to watch the colorful ceremony known as the Trooping of the Colors, which epitomizes the dignity and power of the British empire.

At a luncheon given by the Air Council, Lindbergh was presented with the *Daily Mail's* gold aviation cup, which was instituted many years ago by the late Lord Northcliffe. Here Sir Samuel Hoare was the principal speaker. After complimenting Lindbergh on his flight he continued:

"There are some foolish people—I am glad to think there are very few of them—who are asking you the question: 'Of what use to the world are these efforts and sacrifices? Of what use to the world is a flight like Captain Lindbergh's?' If I had time I should prove to them that from a tech-

NEW YORK CITY'S WELCOME

NEW YORK CITY—A JUNE SNOWSTORM

nical point of view these long distant flights are
of great value. They stimulate progress; they
test reliability.

"Is it not of value to the technical progress of
aviation that a single air cooled engine of 220
H. P., consuming only 10 gallons of petrol an
hour, should have travelled over 3600 miles and
been fit for another lap at the end of this?

"Is not a long distance flight of this kind of
great value as a test of aerial navigation? Flying through fogs and storms, Captain Lindbergh
never seems to have deflected from his course.
Surely this experience is not only a testimony of
his great skill as a navigator but also a lesson in
the study of navigation. But I set aside these
technical justifications, for upon a flight of this
kind the world at large rightly reaches its verdict
upon broader grounds. The peoples of many
countries are today applauding Captain Lindbergh's achievement not so much because some
material gain will be obtained in this or that
way, but because it is a fine example of nerve and

endurance, of skill, courage, enterprise and adventure.

"The more drab the world becomes the more gladly we welcome such fine achievements as his.

"Today therefore I ask you to drink to the health of Captain Lindbergh as the pilot who has broken the world's record, and as a worthy representative of our close friends and war allies, the pilots of the United States of America. Still more, however, do I ask you to drink to his health as a young man who embodies the spirit of adventure and lights up the world with a flash of courage and daring, and, I am glad to say, of success."

In the late afternoon, at the invitation of Lord and Lady Astor, Lindbergh had tea at the House of Commons. That evening the Royal Air Club gave him a dinner at the Savoy. From there he went to a Swedish festival and at midnight attended the famous Derby Eve Ball at Albert Hall. He arrived with the Prince of Wales and as he entered the band struck up

"Yankee Doodle." There he made his shortest speech of many short ones. It was simply: "I thank you for my reception tonight. It has been one of the greatest of my life."

On June 1st Lindbergh saw his first Derby. Three hundred thousand people had travelled to Epsom Downs to see this great traditional spectacle of horse racing. As the visiting flier was guest of Lord Lonsdale he sat in a box surrounded by royalty.

That evening was his last in England's capital. The combined American societies of London entertained him at a banquet. After many speeches, Sir Samuel Hoare rose once more to the occasion and expressed this parting thought:

"Perhaps before long, instead of a single flight, we can induce you to make a regular habit of it. The sooner air communications are established between the two English speaking nations, the better our relations will be. You came to us as a great aviator, but I know you leave as a real friend of England. I am not sure that the latter part of your trip has not been as important as your first.

"It was a triumph of man over machinery, of man over the brute forces of nature. The flight was a tribute to the young men of the world— of the new generation which has sprung up since the war, determined to subdue the forces of na- ture—determined in the near future to make the air a great highway for intercourse between your people and ours."

The day set for departure was misty. On arrival at Kinnerly Airdrome Lindbergh found conditions too difficult to fly to Paris. So there he remained that night as the guest of the Royal Air Force. But he had little sleep; for at 3:30 a messenger awakened him with word the weather was clearing.

He hopped off at 6:20 A.M. but thirty-eight minutes later, due to low visibility, he came down at Lympnel, England. At eight o'clock a big Handley Page mail and passenger plane flew over. Whereupon Lindbergh quickly went aloft and used the big ship as a guide all the way to Le Bourget.

In the afternoon he attended a ceremony at the Swedish Church in Paris and the next morning—Saturday June 5th,—he took off for Cherbourg at 9:22 accompanied by twenty planes.

Just as he was ready to go, Costes and Rignot, the two French aviators who were leaving on their eastward trip in an effort to beat the non-stop record he had established, came over to say goodby and he wished them Godspeed.

On the way to Cherbourg Lindbergh ran into wind, rain, hail and fog. He landed there at 11:35 amid what seemed to be the entire population of the port. He was cordially welcomed by the full staff of city officials. After lunch at the Mayor's château he was motored into the city proper, and at the Gare Maritime a plaque was unveiled commemorating the spot where he had first flown over France on his way to Le Bourget.

To avoid pressure of the crowd he jumped

upon a Cunard tender at the dock and reached the fast launch of Admiral Burrage which carried him to the *U.S.S. Memphis,* ordered by President Coolidge to bring the flier home.

IV

WASHINGTON

I T is probable that when Lindbergh reached America he got the greatest welcome any man in history has ever received; certainly the greatest when judged by numbers; and by far the greatest in its freedom from that unkind emotion which in such cases usually springs from one people's triumph over another.

Lindbergh's victory was all victory; for it was not internecine, but that of our human species over the elements against which for thousands of centuries man's weakness has been pitted.

The striking part of it all was that a composite picture of past homecoming heroes wouldn't look any more like Charles Lindbergh did that day of his arrival in Washington than a hitching post looks like a green bay tree.

Caesar was glum when he came back from
Gaul; Napoleon grim; Paul Jones defiant;
Peary blunt; Roosevelt abrupt; Dewey defer-
ential; Wilson brooding; Pershing imposing.
Lindbergh was none of these. He was a plain
citizen dressed in the garments of an everyday
man. He looked thoroughly pleased, just a
little surprised, and about as full of health and
spirits as any normal man of his age should be.
If there was any wild emotion or bewilderment in
the occasion it lay in the welcoming crowds, and
not in the air pilot they were saluting.

The cruiser *Memphis*, on which Lindbergh
travelled, passed through the Virginia Capes on
her way to Washington a few minutes after five
P.M. of the afternoon of June 10. Here Lindbergh got the first taste of what was to come.

A convoy of four destroyers, two army blimps
from Langley Field and forty airplanes of the
Army, Navy and Marine Corps accompanied
the vessel as she steamed up Chesapeake Bay.
As the night fell they wheeled toward their vari-

ous bases and were soon lost to view. They gave no salute; and, for all the casual observer might have noted, they were merely investigating this newcomer to their home waters. But they left an indelible impression upon those in the *Memphis* that the morrow was to be extraordinary.

Saturday June 11, 1927, dawned hot and clear in Washington. It was evident early in the day that something far out of the city's peaceful summer routine was going to happen. Streets were being roped off. Special policemen were going to their posts. Airplanes flew about overhead. Citizens began gathering in little clumps up and down Pennsylvania Avenue, many seating themselves on fruit boxes and baskets as if for a long wait.

The din that greeted the *Memphis* off Alexandria, suburb of Washington, began the noisy welcome that lasted for several hours. Every roof top, window, old ship, wharf and factory floor was filled with those who simply had to see

Lindbergh come home. Factory whistles, automobiles, church bells and fire sirens all joined in the pandemonium.

In the air were scores of aircraft. One large squadron of nearly fifty pursuit planes maneuvered in and out of the heavy vaporous clouds that hung over the river. Beneath them moved several flights of slower bombers. The giant dirigible airship, the **U.S.S.** *Los Angeles,* wound back and forth above the course of the oncoming *Memphis.*

By eleven o'clock the saluting began. Vice Admiral Burrage, also returning on the *Memphis,* received his customary fifteen guns from the Navy yard. The President's salute of 21 guns was exchanged. Firing from the cruisers' battery and from the shore stations lent a fine rhythmic punctuation to the constantly increasing noise from other quarters.

Just before noon the *Memphis* came alongside the Navy Yard dock and a gangplank was hoisted to her rail. On the shore were collected a notable group of cabinet officers and high officials. There were the Secretary of the Navy, Curtis D. Wilbur; the Secretary of War, Dwight F. Davis; Postmaster General Harry S. New; and former Secretary of State, Charles Evans Hughes. There were Admiral Edward W. Eberle, Chief of Naval Operations; Major General Mason W. Patrick and Rear Admiral William A. Moffett, heads of the Army and Navy air forces. There was Commander Richard E. Byrd who flew to the North Pole, and who later followed Lindbergh's trail to France.

When the gangplank was in place Admiral Burrage came down it and a moment later returned with a lady on his arm. This lady was Mrs. Evangeline Lindbergh, the young pilot's mother.

Instantly a new burst of cheering went up; but many wept—they knew not just why.

For a few minutes mother and son disappeared into a cabin aboard the *Memphis*. It was a nice touch; something more than the brass bands and cheering. And it somehow symbolized a great deal of what was being felt and said that hot morning in our country's great capital.

Next came brief and a somewhat informal greeting by the dignitaries. In their glistening high silk hats they surrounded Lindbergh and for a bit shut him off from the pushing perspiring crowd still held at bay ashore by the bayonets of the marines.

Suddenly the crowd could hold its patience no longer. With one frantic push it broke through the ranks of "Devil Dogs" and swarmed down upon the moored vessel. Trouble was averted by the simple expedient of getting Lindbergh quickly into one of the waiting cars and starting for the Navy Yard gate.

The parade escort had been lined up some hours ahead of time. Now it got under way toward the center of the city, leading the automobiles that carried the official party. Clattering hoofs of cavalrymen, blare of bands and a rolling cheer along the ranks of waiting thousands marked the progress of the young American flier who had so gloriously come home.

Here for the first time Lindbergh saw the spirit in which his people were to greet him. They were curious, yes; crowds always are on such occasions. And they were gay with their handclapping and flag-waving, shouting and confetti throwing. But there was a note of enthusiasm everywhere that transcended just a chorus of holiday seekers witnessing a new form of circus. There was something deeper and finer in the way people voiced their acclaim. Many of them wiped their eyes while they laughed; many stood with expressionless faces, their looks glued upon the face of the lad who had achieved so great a thing and yet seemed to take it all so calmly.

When the parade reached the natural amphitheatre of the Washington Monument the hillsides were jammed with a great gathering of men, women and children. On the high stand that had been erected, the President of the

United States and Mrs. Coolidge waited to receive the man who but three weeks and a day before had been a comparatively unknown adventurer hopping off for Paris by air.

Ranged about the President were the ambassadors of many foreign countries, members of the diplomatic corps with their wives and daughters, and nearly all the high officials of the government.

When Lindbergh mounted the stand the President came forward and grasped his hand. Those closest to Mr. Coolidge say that rarely has he shown the unrestrained cordiality he put into that simple greeting.

The President now moved to the front of the stand and waited for the applause to be stilled. Presently, when the multitude again was quiet, he began slowly to speak:

"My Fellow-Countrymen:

"It was in America that the modern art of flying of heavier-than-air machines was first developed. As the experiments became successful, the airplane was devoted to practical purposes.

It has been adapted to commerce in the transportation of passengers and mail and used for national defense by our land and sea forces.

"Beginning with a limited flying radius, its length has been gradually extended. We have made many flying records. Our Army fliers have circumnavigated the globe. One of our Navy men started from California and flew far enough to have reached Hawaii, but being off his course, landed in the water. Another officer of the Navy has flown to the North Pole. Our own country has been traversed from shore to shore in a single flight.

"It had been apparent for some time that the next great feat in the air would be a continuous flight from the mainland of America to the mainland of Europe. Two courageous Frenchmen made the reverse attempt and passed to a fate that is as yet unknown.

"Others were speeding their preparations to make the trial, but it remained for an unknown youth to attempt the elements and win. It is the same story of valor and victory by a son of the people that shines through every page of American history.

"Twenty-five years ago there was born in Detroit, Michigan, a boy representing the best traditions of this country, of a stock known for its deeds of adventure and exploration.

"His father, moved with a desire for public service, was a member of Congress for several years. His mother, who dowered her son with her own modesty and charm, is with us today. Engaged in the vital profession of school-teaching, she has permitted neither money nor fame to interfere with her fidelity to her duties.

"Too young to have enlisted in the World War, her son became a student at one of the big State universities. His interest in aviation led him to an Army aviation school, and in 1925 he was graduated as an airplane pilot. In November, 1926, he had reached the rank of Captain in the Officers' Reserve Corps.

"Making his home in St. Louis, he had joined

© *Wide World Photos*

NEW YORK CITY—THE PARADE PASSING THROUGH CENTRAL PARK WHERE OVER 400,000 PEOPLE WERE
GATHERED.   A SOLID BANK OF HUMANITY FLANKED OUR PASSAGE

NEW YORK CITY—PARADE IN CENTRAL PARK AS SEEN FROM A NEARBY SKYSCRAPER

the 110th Observation Squadron of the Missouri National Guard. Some of his qualities noted by the Army officers who examined him for promotion, as shown by reports in the files of the Militia Bureau of the War Department, are as follows:

" 'Intelligent,' 'industrious,' 'energetic,' 'dependable,' 'purposeful,' 'alert,' 'quick of reaction,' 'serious,' 'deliberate,' 'stable,' 'efficient,' 'frank,' 'modest,' 'congenial' 'a man of good moral habits and regular in all his business transactions.'

"One of the officers expressed his belief that the young man 'would successfully complete everything he undertakes.' This reads like a prophecy.

"Later he became connected with the United States Mail Service, where he exhibited marked ability, and from which he is now on leave of absence.

"On a morning just three weeks ago yesterday this wholesome, earnest, fearless, courageous product of America rose into the air from **Long** Island in a monoplane christened 'The Spirit of St. Louis' in honor of his home and that **of** his supporters.

"It was no haphazard adventure. **After** months of most careful preparation, supported by a valiant character, driven by an unconquerable will and inspired by the imagination and the spirit of his Viking ancestors, this reserve officer set wing across the dangerous stretches of **the** North Atlantic.

"He was alone. His destination was Paris.

"Thirty-three hours and thirty minutes later, in the evening of the second day, he landed at his destination on the French flying field at Le Bourget. He had traveled over 3,600 miles, and established a new and remarkable record. The execution of his project was a perfect exhibition of his art.

"This country will always remember the way in which he was received by the people of France, by their President and by their Government.

It was the more remarkable because they were mourning the disappearance of their intrepid countrymen, who had tried to span the Atlantic on a western flight.

"Our messenger of peace and good-will had broken down another barrier of time and space and brought two great peoples into closer communion. In less than a day and a half he had crossed the ocean over which Columbus had traveled for sixty-nine days and the Pilgrim Fathers for sixty-six days on their way to the New World.

"But, above all, in showering applause and honors upon this genial, modest American youth, with the naturalness, the simplicity and the poise of true greatness, France had the opportunity to show clearly her goodwill for America and our people.

"With like acclaim and evidences of cordial friendship our Ambassador without portfolio was received by the rulers, the Governments and the peoples of England and Belgium. From other nations came hearty messages of admiration for him and for his country. For these manifold evidences of friendship we are profoundly grateful.

"The absence of self-acclaim, the refusal to become commercialized, which has marked the conduct of this sincere and genuine exemplar of fine and noble virtues, has endeared him to every one. He has returned unspoiled.

"Particularly has it been delightful to have him refer to his airplane as somehow possessing a personality and being equally entitled to credit with himself, for we are proud that in every particular this silent partner represented American genius and industry. I am told that more than 100 separate companies furnished materials, parts or service in its construction.

"And now, my fellow-citizens, this young man has returned. He is here. He has brought his unsullied fame home. It is our great privilege to welcome back to his native land, on behalf of his own people, who have a deep affection for him and have been thrilled by his splendid achievement, a Colonel of the United States Officers' Reserve Corps, an illustrious citizen of our Republic, a conqueror of the air and strengthener of the ties which bind us to our sister nations across the sea.

"And, as President of the United States, I bestow the Distinguished Flying Cross, as a symbol of appreciation for what he is and what he has done, upon Colonel Charles A. Lindbergh."

Upon completing this address the President then conferred upon Lindbergh the Distinguished Flying Cross.

A new burst of cheering went up as the medal was being pinned on by the President. It was at this point in the proceedings that the Secretary of the Navy, ordinarily most placid of men, is alleged to have waved his arm in the air like a college cheer leader and hurrahed as loudly as any. When quiet came again Lindbergh rose and replied to the President. What he said was brief. But had he uttered a hundred times as many words, he could scarcely have conveyed a more important message to those about him.

He said: "On the evening of May 21, I arrived at Le Bourget, France. I was in Paris for one week, in Belgium for a day and was in London and in England for several days. Everywhere I went, at every meeting I attended, I was requested to bring a message home to you. Always the message was the same.

" 'You have seen,' the message was, 'the affection of the people of France for the people of America demonstrated to you. When you return to America take back that message to the people of the United States from the people of France and of Europe.'

"I thank you."

This is no place to dwell upon the minutiæ of that great day. The picture must be sketched in with bold strokes and stippled background. But it is impossible to pass this one short speech of Lindbergh's and not cajole the reader to gather something of its significance. In a sen-

tence it tells the story of the flight; it gives what
the speaker considered his immediate and outstanding achievement; and it phrases that
achievement in words so touching and so eloquent that France and America, half-estranged
through wretched debt, rang with them for days.

The final touch of the miracle was that this
speech was extemporaneous.

Just as when Lincoln finished his Gettysburg
address his listeners sat stunned at the very brevity of it, so was there a curious silence immediately following Lindbergh's utterance.   Then
came long applause.   Hats were not thrown in
the air.   But men and women clapped until their
palms were numb.   Again many wept.   A radio
announcer whose stock-in-trade was routine emotional appeal, broke down and sobbed.

More and more people were beginning to realize that something was happening far greater
than just the celebration of a mechanical triumph
over the ocean separating Europe from America.

The ceremony ended as simply and quickly

as it had begun. The President's own car whisked Lindbergh away to the temporary White House in Dupont Circle. A curious and eager crowd lingered there behind police lines throughout the afternoon. From time to time their demanding cheers could be silenced only by Lindbergh's smiling presence at the door or balcony.

President and Mrs. Coolidge entertained members of the Cabinet and their wives that night. Lindbergh sat on Mrs. Coolidge's right. He wore conventional evening dress and was distinguished by the ease and simplicity with which he met both sallies and inquiries of the imposing guests.

It is one of the cruelties of social lionization that we search for the peculiarities of our specimen. In Lindbergh's case his peculiarity lay in the fact that neither by word, nor look, nor deed was he in any way grotesque. His eyes were clear, his smile quick; like a practised diplomat he eluded entangling discussion; and he had a ready reply for every intelligent inquiry put to him within his range of knowledge or experience.

It is at risk of dampening the ardor of our narrative that we repeatedly point to this trait of simplicity that lies in Lindbergh. We do so because it was from close within the nucleus of this trait that there sprung the incredible emotional reaction towards his personality.

After the President's dinner Lindbergh attended a meeting of the National Press Club in the Washington Auditorium. This was his first public appearance "under roof" in America. Six thousand people risked imminent heat stroke by crowding into every seat and cranny of the building.

The program opened with an address on behalf of the Press Club by Richard V. Oulahan. Because this address illuminated the feelings of the "Fourth Estate," proverbially cynical toward notoriety, we give it here in full:

"In your journalistic flight of the past three weeks," said Mr. Oulahan, "you must have learned that much may be read between the lines of what is printed in newspapers. So even a novice in newspaperdom like yourself would have no trouble in reading between the lines of this journalistic expression an intimate note of sincere affection."

"We of the press rub elbows with all manner of mankind. We see much of good but we see much of self-seeking, of sordid motive, as we sit in the wings watching the world's procession pass across the stage. If it is true that through our contacts we are sprinkled with a coating of the dry dust of cynicism, that dust was blown away in a breath, as it were, when our professional brethren who greeted you overseas broadcast the news of your peerless exploit. To Americans it brought a spontaneous feeling of pride that you were of their nationality.

"The whole world was carried off its feet by an accomplishment so daring, so masterful in execution, so superb in achievement, by the picture presented of that onrushing chariot of dauntless youth, flashing across uncharted heavens straight through the storm's barrage.

"But if the press, with such an inspiration, performed its mission well, it found equal inspiration. It performed as fine a mission in chronicling the subsequent conduct of our young Ambassador of Good Will. His words and bearing dissipated vapors of misunderstanding. He personified, to a Europe amazed at the revelation, the real spirit of America.

"The press should be proud then, if in telling the story of this later phase in the career of the American boy, it brought to the peoples of the world a new realization that clean living, clean thinking, fair play and sportsmanship, modesty of speech and manner, faith in a mother's prayers, have a front page news value intriguing imagination and inviting emulation, and are still potent as fundamentals of success."

Postmaster General New then stepped forward and gave Lindbergh the first special airmail stamp. As he handed it to the flier he said:

"It is as a pilot in the service of the Air Mail that I greet you. There is no public service devoted to the peace time of the public whose past and present are attended by the romance that are attached to the history of the Post Office Department of the United States.

"From the single couriers of the early days, who followed the uncertain trails through wood and fen on horseback and on foot, the picturesque riders of the pony express of a later day, who risked their lives at the hands of savage foes in the wilderness, the drivers who serve amid the rigors of the frozen North with dog teams and sleds, to those intrepid pilots who pierce the night with the air mail and of whom you are a worthy representative, the whole story is set in an atmosphere of most engaging romance.

"It has no titles to bestow—no medal it can add to those that have been given in recognition of your splendid achievement. There is one thing, however, it can do that will everywhere be regarded as most appropriate. It has issued a stamp designed for special use with the air mail which bears your name and a representation of the other member of that very limited partnership in which you made your now famous journey across seas. It is the first time a stamp has been issued in honor of a man still living—a distinction which you have worthily won.

"It is my great pleasure to be privileged to present to you, and to the mother who gave you to this service, the first two copies of this issue as the best evidence of the enduring regard of the Post Office Department of the United States."

These speeches are quoted because better than almost any other capturable entity of those days they reflect the wide scope of the effect Lindbergh's success had on both governmental and business routine. Surely it is difficult to conceive of a military victor shaking so many foundations, no matter what the might of his mailed fist.

Secretary of State Kellogg next presented Lindbergh with a memorial volume consisting of a compilation of diplomatic exchanges between the State Department and the Foreign Offices of the world in connection with the flight. His words lined in a little more of the bewildering picture of the world's admiration unfolding before Lindbergh's frankly astonished gaze.

"Colonel Charles A. Lindbergh," he slowly and ponderously began, staring hard at the object of his eulogy. "On May 20th and 21st, 1927, the world was electrified by the news of your non-stop flight from New York to Paris. It was a marvelous accomplishment requiring the highest courage, skill and self-reliance. Probably no act of a single individual in our day has ever aroused such universal enthusiasm and admiration. Your great deed is a mile-stone marking scientific advancement.

"You have been congratulated by Kings and Presidents. You have listened to the plaudits of thousands and thousands in Europe and you know the tributes which have been justly paid to you by millions more. You do not now realize the thousands who have expressed their congratulations in letters and telegrams. I have had

printed in this little volume only the official telegrams which passed through the Department of
State and I take pleasure in presenting to you
this volume in commemoration of your epochal
achievement.

"Along the highway of human progress, as we
look back over the last half century we marvel
at the progress in science, the arts and invention.
Truly this is a marvelous age and your daring
feat will pass into the pages of history."

Then came Dr. Charles G. Abbott, Acting
Secretary of the Smithsonian Institution who informed Lindbergh that the Institute had decided
to award him the Langley "Medal of Pioneers."
This honor has in the past been bestowed upon
a small but distinguished group such as Orville
Wright, Glenn H. Curtiss and Gustave Eiffel.
Thus was added to the tribute of press and state
the commendation of one of the oldest and finest
scientific bodies in the world.

Followed next a medley of messages from
special organizations. Greetings from cities

touched by Lindbergh in his historic flight from San Diego to Paris were read. St. Louis sent a moving reminder that her people were "waiting for you now impatiently . . . waiting since that gray morning when you launched out over the clouds and the sea for Paris."

There was one from the British Government, something almost without precedent when it is considered that its recipient was a private citizen on a private enterprise. The official bearer read:

"I have been desired by the British Government to express to Colonel Lindbergh on this occasion in behalf of all the people of Great Britain their warm congratulations on the safe return home after his historic flight across the Atlantic. The British people regard Colonel Lindbergh with special admiration and affection not only for his great courage and resource, but also for his equally great modesty in success and generosity in giving their due to other aviators who have gone before."

At the end of this bewildering array of ora-

NEW YORK CITY—SPEAKING AT THE CEREMONIES IN CENTRAL PARK. GOVERNOR SMITH OF NEW YORK
BEHIND THE "MIKE"

BROOKLYN, N. Y.—SPEAKING AT THE CEREMONIES IN PROSPECT PARK

© U. & U.

tions and gifts the speaker of the evening was announced. One has only to put oneself in Lindbergh's place after reading some of the eloquence listed above to admire the moral courage it took to face that huge audience and once more speak with directness and precision of the things nearest his heart—things often furthest from the burden of the discourse:

"I want to express my appreciation of the reception I've met in America and the welcome I have received here tonight." It was plain the flier was going to cover another field than the infinitely delicate one he had touched earlier in the day. "When I landed at Le Bourget a few weeks ago, I landed with the expectancy and hope of being able to see Europe. It was the first time I had ever been abroad. I had seen a number of interesting things when I flew over Ireland and Southern England and France. I had only been gone from America two days or a little less, and I wasn't in any particular hurry to get back.

"But by the time I had been in France a week, Belgium a day and England two or three days —by that time I had opened several cables from America and talked with three Ambassadors and their attachés and found that it didn't make much difference whether I wanted to stay or not: and while I was informed that it was not necessarily an order to come back home, there was a battleship waiting for me.

"The Ambassador said this wasn't an order, but advice," the aviator added.

"So on June 4 I sailed on the *Memphis* from Cherbourg and this morning as I came up the Potomac I wasn't very sorry that I had listened to it.

"There were several things I saw in Europe that are of interest to American aviation. All Europe looks on our air mail service with reverence. There is nothing like it anywhere abroad.

"But, whereas we have mail lines, they have passenger lines. All Europe is covered with a network of lines carrying passengers between all the big cities. Now it is up to us to create and develop passenger lines that compare with our mail routes. For this we have natural advantages in the great distances here that lend themselves to rapid transportation by air. Moreover, we can make these long trips without the inconvenience of passing over international boundaries.

"The question comes up, 'Why has Europe got ahead of us in commercial air lines?' The reason is, of course, that the Governments over there give subsidies. I don't think we want any subsidies over here. Of course, if we had them they would create passenger lines overnight, so to speak, but in the long run the air lines, the distance they covered and the routes would be controlled entirely by the subsidies.

"What we need now more than any other one thing is a series of airports in every city and town throughout the United States. Given these airports, in a very few years the nations of Europe would be looking toward our passenger lines as they now look at our mail routes."

Sunday was another full day. Under able guidance of the Chief Executive, Lindbergh did the things every good American would expect him to do. And, as one who has seen the lad at close range, we can say that he did them gladly and with profound appreciation for the privilege of doing them. After you come to know him you find out that's the kind he is.

He went to church with President and Mrs. Coolidge. Accompanied by his mother he laid a wreath upon the tomb of the Unknown Soldier in the great memorial amphitheatre in Arlington Cemetery. He drove to Georgetown and visited the wounded soldiers at Walter Reed Hospital. He attended a celebration in honor of the 150th anniversary of the American flag, for which services were held on the steps of the Capitol and presided over by Charles Evans Hughes.

It was at this last ceremony that Lindbergh received the Cross of Honor. His response to the honor was brief and typically to the point. He declared that credit for his flight should "not go to the pilot alone but to American science and genius which had given years of study to the advancement of aeronautics."

"Some things should be taken into consideration in connection with our flight that have not heretofore been given due weight. That is just what made this flight possible. It was not the act of a single pilot. It was the culmination of twenty years of aeronautical research and the assembling together of all that was practicable and best in American aviation. It represented American industry.

"In addition to this consideration should be given the scientific researches that have been in progress for countless centuries. All of this should have consideration in apportioning credit for the flight. Credit should go not alone to the pilot, but to the other factors that I have briefly enumerated. I thank you."

This was the day well worthy of what Lindbergh had done and what he stood for. And again, by the spiritual values it comprised, it struck the inspirational note which had dominated almost everything the lad has done or said from the moment of his landing at Le Bourget to the moment of this writing.

Is it any wonder that the populace responded as it did?

V

O N Monday morning, June 13, Lindbergh rose at dawn and reached the May-flower Hotel at 6:45 A.M. for breakfast with the National Aeronautical Association, which conferred a life membership upon him.

He reached Bolling Field outside Washington at about 7:30 A.M. Here rose the only incident to mar his otherwise flawless happiness in the welcome he had received. His plane refused to "mote." It didn't actually rebel. But there was sufficient irregularity in its engine to discourage him from risking delay when New York City was almost every minute voicing its impatience that he hurry to the celebration awaiting him there. A pursuit plane was quickly obtained from an army field and he was soon in the air with his escort of more than a score of ships.

The course of the group led them over Baltimore, Wilmington and Philadelphia. Eyewitnesses later reported that demonstrations took place at every one of these places as the air cavalcade went by. Of course those in the planes, thousands of feet in the air and deafened by the roar of their motors, heard nothing of the bells and whistles that saluted them as they passed.

Lindbergh arrived at Mitchel Field about noon. As he had flown in a land plane and was to be met in the lower harbor by the mayor's yacht, he had to make a quick change to an amphibian. This ship happened to be the *San Francisco* which had but recently returned from her "good will" flight to South America.

She took off from dry land and a few minutes later volplaned down to the water just above the Narrows.

Here a sight met Lindbergh's eyes that old harbor inhabitants declare was absolutely without precedent in the marine annals of New York. Even the famous Hudson-Fulton Exposition with its vast water parades and maneuvers was exceeded.

In the sparkling sunshine of a perfect June

morning was gathered half a thousand vessels of every kind and description. Excursion boats, yachts, tugs, motor boats, launches, fireboats, even dredges, formed the spectacular array of shipping gathered to meet the man who had made the proudest of surface craft, the ocean liner, a back number on the sea.

A police launch swung up to the *San Francisco* and took Lindbergh aboard. He was brought to the *Macom*, yacht of the Mayor of New York, amid a deafening chorus of whistles. Indeed, so great was the din that conversation among the welcoming committees was quite impossible and remained so throughout the hour's voyage to the Battery.

As the *Macom* moved forward the huge disorderly fleet of crowding vessels swung into rough column behind her. Massive ocean going tugs and fireboats clung close aboard to guard her from too curious craft who sought to wedge their way in toward the yacht for a better look at the bare-headed boy standing atop her pilot house.

As in Washington, the air was well filled with planes. Their motors' roar lent a sort of solemn undertone to the shrieking chorus of whistles and sirens.

There was an interview below decks. It was not very successful. The whistles made too much noise and Lindbergh very properly refused to discuss his "feelings", which are meat and drink to the writing man.

It was estimated that 300,000 people were massed in the vicinity of the Battery when the *Macom* hove alongside. Lining the streets clear to Central Park was a multitude that was variously estimated from 3,000,000 to 4,500,000. Scores of people were in their places before eight A.M. on upper Fifth Avenue. Lindbergh did not pass them until three P.M. Traffic was disrupted. Police control was strained to its utmost.

As evidence of the almost unanimous turnout for the occasion the Police Department of the City issued special instructions to all citizens about leaving their houses protected against thieves, something that hadn't been done for a generation.

When the cavalcade with Lindbergh leading started up Broadway there came the famous New York "snow storm" consisting of a myriad paper bits and confetti streamers floating downward from the skyscrapers. Photographs do scant justice to the spectacle.

At the City Hall Mayor Walker expressed the city's sentiments with a felicity that deserves their record here. He spoke more informally than most had spoken in Washington; by the same token he echoed through his easily forgivable eloquence much that the inarticulate thousands waiting without the lines would like to have said.

He struck right at the heart of things when he began:

"Let me dispense with any unnecessary official side or function, Colonel, by telling you that if you have prepared yourself with any letters of introduction to New York City they are not necessary.

"Everybody all over the world, in every language, has been telling you and the world about yourself. You have been told time after time where you were born, where you went to school, and that you have done the supernatural thing of an air flight from New York to Paris. I am

satisfied that you have become convinced of it
by this time.

"And it is not my purpose to reiterate any of
the wonderful things that have been so beautifully spoken and written about you and your
triumphal ride across the ocean. But while it
has become almost axiomatic, it sometimes seems
prosaic to refer to you as a great diplomat, because after your superhuman adventure, by your
modesty, by your grace, by your gentlemanly
American conduct, you have left no doubt of that.
But the one thing that occurs to me that has been
overlooked in all the observations that have been
made of you is that you are a great grammarian,
and that you have given added significance and
a deeper definition to the word 'we.'

"We have heard, and we are familiar with, the
editorial 'we,' but not until you arrived in Paris
did we learn of the aeronautical 'we.' Now you
have given to the world a flying pronoun.

"That 'we' that you used was perhaps the only
word that would have suited the occasion and the
great accomplishment that was yours. That
all-inclusive word 'we' was quite right, because
you were not all alone in the solitude of the sky

and the sea, because every American heart, from
the Atlantic to the Pacific, was beating for you.
Every American, every soul throughout the
world, was riding with you in spirit, urging you
on and cheering you on to the great accomplishment that is yours.

"That 'we' was a vindication of the courage,
of the intelligence, of the confidence and the
hopes of Nungesser and Coli, now only alive in
the prayers and the hearts of the people of the
entire world. That 'we' that you coined was
well used, because it gave an added significance
and additional emphasis to the greatest of any
and all ranks, the word of faith, and turned the
hearts of all the people of the civilized world to
your glorious mother, whose spirit was your
spirit, whose confidence was your confidence,
and whose pride was your pride; the 'we' that in-
cludes all that has made the entire world stand
and gasp at your great feat, and that 'we' also
sent out to the world another message and
brought happiness to the people of America, and
admiration and additional popularity for America and Americans by all the peoples of the
European countries.

"Colonel Lindbergh, on this very platform are the diplomatic corps, the diplomatic representatives of all the countries of the civilized world; but before you and around you are the peoples themselves of all the countries of the civilized world, foregathered in this city, the greatest cosmopolitan institution in all the world; the peoples who have come from the forty-eight States of the Union and from every country of the civilized world; and here today, as Chief Magistrate of this city, the world city, the gateway to America, the gateway through which peoples from the world have come in the search for liberty and freedom—and have found it—here today let it be written and let it be observed that the Chief Magistrate of this great city, the son of an immigrant, is here to welcome as the world's greatest hero, another son of an immigrant.

"What more need I call to your attention, in view of the busy life that you have been leading and have the right to expect to lead? What more can we say as we foregather in the streets of this old city? And today, not by the words alone of the Mayor, or the beautifully written words of a scroll, as you stand here I am sure you hear something even more eloquent and glorious. You can hear the heart-beats of six millions of people that live in this the City of New York. And the story they tell is one of pride, is one of admiration for courage and intelligence; is one that has been born out of and is predicated upon the fact that as you went over the ocean you inscribed on the heavens themselves a beautiful rainbow of hope and courage and confidence in mankind.

"Colonel Lindbergh, New York City is yours —I don't give it to you; you won it. New York not only wants me to tell you of the love and appreciation that it has for your great venture, but is deeply and profoundly grateful for the fact that again you have controverted all the old rules and made new ones of your own, and kind of cast aside temporarily even the weather prophets, and have given us a beautiful day.

"So, just another word of the happiness, the distinction and the pride which the City of New York has today to find you outside this historical building, sitting side by side with your glorious mother, happy to find you both here, that we might have the opportunity and a close-up, to tell you that like the rest of the world—but because we are so much of the world, even with a little greater enthusiasm than you might find in any other place in the world—I congratulate you and welcome you into the world city, that you may look the world in the face."

Mayor Walker pinned the Medal of Valor upon the lapel of Lindbergh's coat. Whereupon Lindbergh for the first time gave in some detail his sense of the size of the welcome he had received:

"When I was preparing to leave New York, I was warned that if we landed at Le Bourget we might receive a rather demonstrative reception. After having an hour of Le Bourget I did not believe that anyone in New York had the slightest conception of what we did receive. Again, at Brussels and at London. At London thirteen hundred of the pride of Scotland Yard were lost in the crowd at Croydon as though they had been dropped in the middle of the ocean. With the exception of a few around the car and around the plane, I never saw more than two at any one time.

"At Washington I received a marvelous recep-

"THE SPIRIT OF ST. LOUIS" AFTER HER RETURN

MITCHEL FIELD, L. I.——AFTER THE FLIGHT TO WASHINGTON

tion. But at New York I believe that all four put together would be in about just the position of those London bobbies."

"When I landed at Le Bourget I landed looking forward to the pleasure of seeing Europe and the British Isles. I learned to speak of Europe and the British Isles after I landed in London. I had been away from America a little less than two days. I had been very interested in the things I saw while passing over southern England and France, and I was not in any hurry to get back home.

"By the time I had spent about a week in France and a short time in Belgium and England, and had opened a few cables from the United States, I found that I did not have much to say about how long I would stay over there."

Lindbergh paused for the laughter to subside. This point always tickled people greatly.

"So I left Europe and the British Isles with the regret that I had been unable to see either Europe or the British Isles. When I started up the Potomac from the *Memphis* I decided that I was not so sorry that I had taken the

Ambassador's advice. After spending about an hour in New York I know I am not."

The parade now formed again and moved up Broadway, through Lafayette Street, to Ninth and over to Fifth. At Madison Square it halted at the Shaft of Eternal Light. The ceremony was touching and impressive. The tall shaft topped by a crystal star, imprisoning light everlasting, was a fitting memorial to the men who gave up their lives in the World War. Lindbergh here laid a wreath in their memory.

Fifth Avenue had been packed with people since morning. It was now mid-afternoon. As in Washington a wave of cheering marked the progress of the car which held the city's guest of honor.

At St. Patrick's Cathedral he stopped, got out of his automobile and met Cardinal Hayes.

In Central Park the official city welcome ended amid a gathering estimated at above 300,000 people. Bands were playing and automobile horns added to the din.

Governor Smith of New York was waiting there with his staff on a specially built reviewing stand. He pinned on Lindbergh the State Medal

of Honor: adding again to the ever lengthening
list of honors. There was again an exchange of
speeches met by salvos of applause. A sky writer
wrote "Hail Lindy" high in the air. Policemen
wrestled with swaying crowds. More than on
the avenue it seemed as if the city were concentrated for a Lindbergh it would never forget.

Near five the great demonstration came to
an end. For a few hours the center of attraction could escape to the refuge that had been
prepared for him and his mother in a private
apartment. But this escape was qualified by the
fact that it took a large guard to hold in check
the many people who sought access to Lindbergh
for one reason or another.

At. 8:15 P.M. he rode out on Long Island to
the beautiful estate of Clarence Mackay, head
of the Postal Telegraph Company. The place
had been transformed into a fairyland of colored
Japanese lanterns, fountains and illuminated
shrubbery. Eighty of New York's most prominent people attended the dinner which was
kingly in its appointments. Later several hundred guests came in for dancing.

It would have seemed that this first terrific day might have exhausted the ardor of the city's welcome. But there followed a kaleidoscopic week that was, if anything, more trying. Not only did Lindbergh move amid a growing chorus of business offers, but his social engagements jammed tighter and tighter as the hours passed. Moreover, his plane was still in Washington, although he was scheduled to fly it to St. Louis for the week-end.

The City of New York gave Lindbergh a dinner of some 4000 guests at the Hotel Commodore. It was there that Mr. Hughes spoke the following unique tribute:

"When a young man, slim and silent, can hop overnight to Paris and then in the morning telephone his greetings to his mother in Detroit; when millions throughout the length and breadth of this land and over sea through the mysterious waves, which have been taught to obey our command, can listen to the voice of the President of the United States according honors for that achievement, honors which are but a faint reflection of the affection and esteem cherished in all hearts for our countryman of the West who dis-

tinguished America by that flight, then indeed
is the day that hath no equal; then is the most
marvelous day that this old earth has ever
known.

"We measure heroes as we do ships by their
displacement. Colonel Lindbergh has displaced
everything. His displacement is beyond all cal-
culation. He fills all our thought; he has displaced politics, Governor Smith.

"For the time being, he has lifted us into the
freer and upper air that is his home. He has
displaced everything that is petty; that is sordid;
that is vulgar. What is money in the presence of
Charles A. Lindbergh?

"What is the pleasure of the idler in the presence of this supreme victor of intelligence and
industry? He has driven the sensation mongers
out of the temples of our thought. He has kin-
dled anew the fires on the eight ancient altars of
that temple. Where are the stories of crime, of
divorce, of the triangles that are never equa-
lateral? For the moment we have forgotten.
This is the happiest day, the happiest day of all
days for America, and as one mind she is now
intent upon the noblest and the best. America is

picturing to herself youth with the highest aims, with courage unsurpassed; science victorious. Last and not least, motherhood, with her loveliest crown.

"We may have brought peoples together. This flight may have been the messenger of good will, but good will for its beneficent effects depends upon the character of those who cherish it.

"We are all better men and women because of this exhibition in this flight of our young friend. Our boys and girls have before them a stirring, inspiring vision of real manhood. What a wonderful thing it is to live in a time when science and character join hands to lift up humanity with a vision of its own diginity.

"There is again revealed to us, with a startling suddenness, the inexhaustible resources of our national wealth. From an unspoiled home, with its traditions of industry, of frugality and honor, steps swiftly into our gaze this young man, showing us the unmeasured treasures in our mines of American character.

"America is fortunate in her heroes; her soul feeds upon their deeds; her imagination revels in their achievements. There are those who would rob them of something of their lustre, but no one can debunk Lindbergh, for there is no bunk about him. He represents to us, fellow-Americans, all that we wish—a young American at his best."

Only by reducing this record to catalog form could it possibly be made to include a fully detailed description of Lindbergh's four amazing days in New York. Every night there was a banquet. Every day there was a festive lunch. Not hundreds, but thousands attended these entertainments; and at the speaker's table there always sat distinguished men whose names were household words among Americans.

Lindbergh spoke at every banquet. Recurrently he paid gracious thanks to those who had helped make his visit such a gorgeous success; he usually ended by speaking on behalf of aviation, the welfare of which he never forgot even in the most crowded moments of his days.

The Merchants' Association gave him a gigantic luncheon. The Aeronautical Chamber of Commerce entertained him at a banquet that filled to overflowing the famous ball room of the Waldorf.

On Wednesday night he gave an exhibition of his endurance that once more reminded the world it was fêting no ordinary hero. After dining on Rodman Wanamaker's yacht and seeing a special performance of a light opera, Lindbergh attended a charity benefit at one of the big theatres. About 1:30 A.M. he escaped through a back door and hurried to Mitchel field. Although still in his evening clothes he borrowed a helmet and hopped off for Washington at 3:05 A.M. By 7:30 A.M. he was back in New York with his own plane.

His last day was too crowded for him to take a nap after his sleepless night. He went to Brooklyn where above a million people gave him another moving welcome. He kept a public luncheon date. He attended a large tea and reception at the Hotel Brevoort where Raymond Orteig presented him with the $25,000 prize that had long stood for the first flight from New York to Paris. At eight, a little tired but still as fresh looking as ever, he followed Charles Schwab in speaking before a massed aviation banquet that included many leading pilots of the world.

© *Wide World Photos*

ST. LOUIS' WELCOME—LOOKING DOWN WASHINGTON AVENUE

MOTHER AND SON

VI

A T 8:17 A.M., Friday June 17th, Lindbergh hopped off in his plane for St. Louis. At Paterson he passed over the plant of the Wright Aeronautical Corporation where had been built the motor that had taken him across the Atlantic. At 11:16 he reached Columbus, Ohio. At Dayton he was joined by an escort of thirty fast Army planes. They took off from the field where the old hangar of Orville and Wilbur Wright still stands.

About 5 P.M. he approached St. Louis in a wet fog. He dropped lower and circled the city. As at New York the sky was dotted with planes. Streets and house tops were massed with people. As he landed at Lambert Field a cordon of troops protected him from the eager crowds.

For the evening he managed to escape to the

home of a friend where he got a little much-
needed rest, though reporters and business so-
licitors still swarmed about him. Saturday
morning came the huge city parade with luncheon and banquet to follow. Sunday he gave an
exhibition flight over the old World's Fair
grounds. Not an hour, scarcely a waking minute,
was he free from demands upon his time and
attention.

By this time his mail had exceeded the wildest
imagination. It was estimated that more than
2,000,000 letters and several hundred thousand
telegrams were sent him. He gave out the following statement:

"To the Press: As an air mail pilot I deeply
appreciate the sentiment which actuated my
countrymen to welcome me home by 'air mail,'
and regret only that I have no way in which to
acknowledge individually every one of the tens
of thousands of 'air mail' greetings I have received, for my heart is in the 'air mail' service,
and I would like to help keep alive the air-con-
sciousness of America which my good fortune
may have helped to awaken."

By this time statisticians began to get busy.

One official association estimated that the tremendous increase of interest in flying developed by Lindbergh's feat caused publications in the United States to use 25,000 tons of newsprint in addition to their usual consumption.

Roughly 5,000 poems were believed to have been written to commemorate the first New York to Paris flight. A town was named "Lindbergh." Scores of babies were reported christened after the flier. An enormous impetus was given the use of air mail.

Inspired editorials were written in every part of the civilized world. The following from the *New York Times* suitably completes this very superficial record of the early Lindbergh welcome by mankind:

"Such a man is one in a host. In treating of the psychology of those who adore Lindbergh it must first be set down that he has the qualities of heart and head that all of us would like to possess. When he left Newfoundland behind, the dauntless fellow seemed to have a rendezvous with Death, but his point of view was that he had an engagement in Paris. Two gallant Frenchmen had lost their lives, it was believed, in an attempt to fly across the Atlantic to the United States. An American, unknown to fame, in whom no one but himself believed, made the passage smoothly, swiftly and surely, traveling alone and almost unheralded. From New York to Paris, without a hand to clasp or a face to look into, was a deed to lose one's head over. And that's what everybody in France, Belgium and England proceeded to do.

"After all, the greater was behind—the young fellow's keeping his own head when millions hailed him as hero, when all the women lost their hearts to him, and when decorations were pinned on his coat by admiring Governments. Lindbergh had the world at his feet, and he blushed like a girl! A more modest bearing, a more unaffected presence, a manlier, kindlier, simpler character no idol of the multitude ever displayed. Never was America prouder of a son."

THE END